Fasting Changed
My Life

Fasting Changed My Life

Andy Anderson

Broadman Press/Nashville, Tennessee

Dewey Decimal Classification: 248.2
Subject Heading: FASTING
Library of Congress Catalog Card Number: 77-82404
Printed in the United States of America

Dedication

To the apples of my eye, and the joys
of my heart, my three wonderful children—
Mary Anne, Ron, and Sonja—
I dedicate this book.

Their lives were not always easy, growing
up as P.K.'s (Preacher's Kids), but today
they shine as polished jewels.
I am, of all men, most blessed.

Appetite Page

HERE IS A BOOK THAT WILL HELP YOU TO:

Understand what the Bible teaches about fasting—
What is a fast? Under what circumstances should people fast? How long should people fast? What will the fast do for people?

Grasp what medical science says about fasting—
Will a fast injure health? Will it cure arthritis, high blood pressure, diabetes, or lower cholesterol levels? Is there a physical benefit?

Learn what others think of fasting—
What do outstanding religious and medical leaders say about fasting?

Lose weight by fasting—
What is one of the most successful weight-loss programs? How can people lose two or more pounds per day without side effects? Are you interested in discovering a spiritual, mental, emotional, and physical exhilaration you've never felt before?

Discipline your life—

Become spiritually healthier—

Discover a new peace and confidence—

Find an unbelievable strength to overcome temptations—

Discover the will of God for your life—
but

Realize there are some cautions.

Foreword

I choose books first by author and then by title. Some authors I read regardless of the title. In other instances titles, regardless of authors, attract me. Then, on rare occasions, there comes a book whose author and title equally appeal to me. Andy Anderson and *Fasting Changed My Life* comprise just such a case!

I have been interested for a long time in the subject of fasting and believe that all serious Christians should look into it with a view to practicing it. I am glad that Andy Anderson has done this for us. We have needed someone as a "trailblazer" in this area—not so much one to be only theoretical and not so much the other to be unsupported.

Here is an interestingly written treatise which is sound and sensible, practical and personal.

I know Andy Anderson. Yet, our total time together has been only a few hours. He is one you can get to know that quickly! I have heard him preach on fasting, and his words were helpful.

I am certain that every reader would welcome some changes in varying areas of his or her life. The reading of this book may change your life, just as the subject matter affected Andy Anderson! Such change is always a welcome prospect.

I predict for this book a wide and happy reception and plan to keep it handy for rereading and continued reference.

JACK R. TAYLOR
PRESIDENT, DIMENSIONS IN CHRISTIAN LIVING

San Antonio, Texas

Contents

Introduction: A New Plateau

This is the personal testimony of my experiences with fasting.

This is not a complete theological, biblical, or experimental study of the subject. However, I believe it is the most complete document on fasting at the time of this writing.

When I became deeply interested in fasting, I could not find a book that contained biblical answers to my questions. So, as a reporter would do, I set out to find out who fasted, what prompted them to fast, where they fasted, why they fasted, and how they fasted. I was intrigued with the anticipation of investigating this mysterious subject.

Being a student of biography and history, I knew that many of the saints who changed human history were great pray-ers and fast-ers. For instance:

In his book *With Christ in the School of Prayer,* ANDREW MURRAY, a pray-er-revivalist, says:

Prayer needs fasting for its full growth. Prayer is the one hand with which we grasp the invisible; fasting, the other with which we let loose and cast away the visible. In nothing is man more closely connected with the world of sense than in his need of food, and his enjoyment of it. It was the fruit, good for food, with which man was tempted and fell in Paradise. It was with bread to be made of stones that Jesus, when He hungered, was tempted in the wilderness, and in fasting that He triumphed. The body has been redeemed to be a temple of the Holy Spirit; it is in body as well as spirit, it is very specially, Scripture says, in eating and drinking, we are to glorify God. It is to be feared that there are many Christians to whom this eating to the glory of God has not become a spiritual reality. And the first thought suggested by Jesus' words in regard to fasting and prayer is that it is only in a life of moderation and temperance and self-denial that there will be the heart or the strength to pray much.

But then there is also its more literal meaning. Sorrow and anxiety cannot eat: joy celebrates its feasts with eating and drinking. There may come times of intense desire, when it is strongly felt how the body, with its appetites, lawful though they be, still hinder the spirit in its battle with the powers of darkness, and the need is felt of keeping it under. We are creatures of the senses: our mind is helped by what comes to us embodied in concrete form; fasting helps to express, to deepen, and to confirm the resolution that we are ready to sacrifice anything, to sacrifice ourselves, to attain what we seek for the kingdom of God. And He who accepted the fasting and sacrifice of the Son knows to value and accept and reward with spiritual power the soul that is thus ready to give up all for Christ and His kingdom.[1]

Murray further states:

Learn from these men (those at the church at Antioch—Acts 13) that the work of the Holy Ghost commands us to new fasting and prayer, to new separation from the spirit and the pleasures of the world, to new consecration to God and to His fellowship. These men gave themselves up to fasting and prayer, and if in all our ordinary Christian work there were more prayer, there would be more blessing in our own inner life.[2]

DAVID BRAINERD, missionary, told of his experiences:

When I return home and give myself to meditation, prayer,

and fasting, my soul longs for mortification, self-denial, humility and divorcement from all things of the world. I have nothing to do with earth, but only labor in it honestly for God. I do not desire to live one minute for anything which earth can afford.[3]

Brainerd's diary is full and monotonous with the record of his sessions of fasting, meditation, and retirement. As he sought God's personal help, he wrote:

Feeling somewhat of the sweetness of communion with God and the constraining force of His love and how admirably it captivates the soul and makes all the desires and affections to center in God, I set apart this day for secret fasting and prayer to God, to direct and bless me with regard to the great work which I have in view of preaching the Gospel and to ask that the Lord would return to me and show me the light of His countenance. I had little life and power in the forenoon. Near the middle of the afternoon God enabled me to wrestle ardently in intercession for my absent friends, but just at night the Lord visited me marvelously in prayer. I think my soul was never in such agony before. I felt no restraint, for the treasures of divine grace were opened to me. I wrestled for absent friends, for the ingathering of souls, for multitudes of poor souls, and for many I thought were the children of God, personally in many places. I was in such agony from sun half an hour high till near dark that I was all over wet with sweat, but yet it seemed to me I had done nothing; oh, my dear Saviour did sweat blood for poor souls! I longed for more compassion toward them. I felt still in a sweet frame, under a sense of divine love and grace, and went to bed in such a frame, with my heart set on God.[4]

R. A. TORREY the world-renowned evangelist, wrote:

How shall we attain an earnestness in prayer? Not by trying to work ourselves up into it. The true method is explained in Romans 8:26, "And in like manner the Spirit also helpeth our infirmity: for we know not how to pray as we ought; but the Spirit Himself maketh intercession for us with groanings which cannot be uttered" (ASV). The earnestness we work up in the energy of the flesh is a repulsive thing. The earnestness wrought in us by the power of the Holy Spirit is pleasing to God. Here, again, if we would pray aright, we must look to the Spirit of God to teach us to pray. It is in this connection that fasting comes. In Daniel 9:3 we read that Daniel set his face "unto the Lord God, to seek by prayer and supplications, with fasting, and sackcloth, and ashes" (KJV). There are those who think that fasting belongs to the old dispensation; but when we look at Acts 14:23 and Acts 13:2-3, we find that it was practiced by the earnest men of the apostolic day. If we would pray with power, we should pray with fasting. This, of course, does not mean that we should fast everytime we pray; but there are times of emergency or special crisis in work or in our individual lives, when men of downright earnestness will withdraw themselves even from the gratification of natural appetites that would be perfectly proper under other circumstances, that they may give themselves up wholly to prayer. There is a peculiar power in such prayer. Every great crisis in life and work should be met that way. There is nothing pleasing to God in our giving up in a purely Pharisaic and legal way things which are pleasant, but there is power in that downright earnestness and determination to obtain in prayer the things of which we sorely feel our need, that leads us to put away everything, even things in themselves most right and necessary, that we may set our faces to find God, and obtain blessings from Him.[5]

JOHN WESLEY, recorded in his diary his seasons of fasting:

Tuesday, March 6 (Bristol),—I began writing a short French grammar. We observed Wednesday 7 as a day of fasting and prayer.[6]

O. HALLESBY stated that fasting is a "live question":

Jesus did not abolish fasting; he lifted it from the legalism of the Old Covenant into the freedom of the New. Fasting is an outward act which should be carried out only when there is an inner need of it (Matt. 9:14-15). Furthermore, Jesus warns against fasting as a means of displaying piety, so as to be seen of men (Matt. 6:16-18).

But should we fast?

This is no doubt a live question in the minds of many Christians in our day. Many look upon fasting as a part of the outward ceremonialism which belonged only to the Old Covenant, and which the Catholics have incorporated into their legalistic system of work-righteousness. That free, evangelical Christians should fast is entirely strange and foreign to their way of thinking.

It is no doubt high time that we feeble, weak-willed and pleasure-loving Christians begin to see what the Scriptures say concerning this element in our sanctification and in our prayer life.

Fasting is not confined to abstinence from eating and drinking. Fasting really means voluntary abstinence for a time from various necessities of life such as food, drink, sleep, rest, association with people and so forth.

The purpose of such abstinence for a longer or shorter period of time is to loosen to some degree the ties which bind us to the world of material things and our surroundings as a whole, in order that we may concentrate all our spiritual powers upon the unseen and eternal things.

To strive in prayer means in the final analysis to take up the battle against all the inner and outward hindrances which would dissociate us from the spirit of prayer.

It is at this point that God has ordained fasting as a means of carrying on the struggle against the subtle and dangerous hindrances which confront us in prayer.

Fasting must be voluntary, Jesus said.[7]

CHARLES FINNEY wrote that a period of fasting for him meant a time when he overhauled his religious life:

I was also led into a state of great dissatisfaction with my own want of stability in faith and love . . . I often felt myself weak in the presence of temptation and needed frequently to hold days of fasting and prayer and to spend much time in overhauling my own religious life in order to retain that communion with God and that hold upon the Divine truth that would enable me efficiently to labor for the promotion of revivals of religion.[8]

MARTIN LUTHER'S biographer, Roland Bainton, wrote:

He fasted sometimes three days on end without a crumb. The seasons of fasting were more consoling to him than those of feasting. Lent was more comforting than Easter.[9]

HENRY MARTYN considered that he had dedicated too much time to public ministry and too little to private communion with God. He was much impressed with the need of setting apart times to fast and to devote times for solemn prayer. He lamented that his lack "of private devotional reading and shortness of prayer through incessant sermon-making had produced much strangeness between God and his soul."[10]

In his book *Power Through Prayer,* E. M. BOUNDS said:

It would not do to say that preachers study too much. Some of them do not study at all; others do not study enough. Numbers do not study the right way to show themselves workmen approved of God. But our great lack is not in head culture, but in heart culture; not in lack of knowledge, but lack of holiness is our sad and telling defect—not that we know too much, but that we do not meditate on God and His Word and watch and fast and pray enough.[11]

Why was it that I had to revert to the last generation of Christians to find fast-ers? Are there no modern leaders whose life-style is fasting?

At that particular time in my life, I had to admit that I knew of no one. Now that I have searched, I have found a few—but, oh, so few.

However, when I discover a person who does fast, I witness an unusually strong person—both with God and man. I have interviewed some of these people and have recorded their responses in chapter 5 of this book.

I travel about 200,000 miles a year as an ACTION Promotion Specialist of The Sunday School Board of the Southern Baptist Convention, and I speak to tens of thousands of people. In looking for those who fast, I have asked many of my audiences if those practicing the habit of fasting would identify themselves. Several dozen have indicated they fasted at least once, but very few have stated that they fast as a way of life.

I concluded early in my search that fasting is a biblical teaching that has remained practically unpracticed in this part of the twentieth century.

In my conferences throughout America I often share my experiences and discoveries with fasting. This has provoked in my audiences a previously unspoken desire to know more about the subject. I write this book in answer to the requests of many Christians who have encouraged me to place my findings in writing. What I write here is the result of a five-year search and experience. Already several personal benefits have become evident. These I will discuss in detail in chapter 6.

1. I am spiritually cleaner. No, I have not arrived; I have only begun in the journey toward holiness.

2. I have learned a new discipline. No longer is my life centered around food and drink. Before the experiences of the last five years, I was a food addict. I ate whether I was hungry or not. It was difficult to go to bed without a snack, but I have realized that life is more than satisfying the physical cravings.

3. I have discovered a more effective prayer life.

4. I have found a previously unknown peace and confidence.

5. I have found an almost unbelievable strength to overcome temptations.

When I began to fast I was afraid to mention my interest for fear people would get the idea that I was becoming a fanatic. But my hunger to "know him, and the power of his resurrection, and the fellowship of his sufferings" (Phil. 3:10) so consumed me that it didn't matter what others thought. I had to discover it for myself.

I was also faced with the problem of how to handle the warning of Jesus, "Moreover when ye fast, be not as the hypocrites, of a sad countenance: for they disfigure their faces, that they may appear unto men to fast. Verily I say unto you, They have their reward. But thou, when thou fastest, anoint thine head, and wash thy face; That thou appear not unto men to fast, but unto thy Father which is in secret: and thy Father which seeth in secret shall reward thee openly" (Matt. 6:16-18).

Should I speak about my fasting? What was I to do at home? How was I to explain my feelings to my wife and children, as close as we were? What was I to do while traveling throughout the nation when my hosts wanted to entertain me in their city's finest restaurants or, even better, in their homes? Right or wrong, my solution has been to give a simple statement that I am fasting—with little or no further comment.

In Matthew 6, where Jesus discussed almsgiving (1-4), praying (5-15), and fasting (16-18), he emphasized that the proper attitude must be maintained. If almsgiving, praying, or fasting is practiced boastfully, there is no reward.

During a fast, I make it my plan not to discuss it. Following a fast, I discuss it only with an attitude of awe that God would allow me to experience such cleansing and peace. The right motives and attitudes are imperative.

The ultimate purpose of this work is to help others know Jesus as Savior and Lord. It is not my ambition to encourage every reader to become a fast-er. I only share my testimony. The use of the personal pronoun will abound throughout this book. It is because this is a personal, not a theoretical, testimony.

ANDY ANDERSON

Fort Myers, Florida

1 I Discovered Fasting For Myself

I grew up in a Christian home in Cheraw, South Carolina. My dad, Stanley Anderson, was born and reared in Chase City, Virginia. He moved to South Carolina to manage a crate factory. There he met a young schoolteacher, Lillie Henrietta Jane Sherrill. Following a beautiful courtship, they married and moved to Church Street, where they lived in a large, two-story, red-roofed house that was to be filled with sons.

Stanley was a Southern Baptist. He became a follower of Jesus and a church member before moving south. Lillie, a native of Cheraw, had grown up in a dedicated Christian home. She joined the Methodist Church as a young girl. In 1971, following her death, I found a paper on which she had written her personal testimony: "I did not really begin to live until I was born again, which took place in my teens; but I was never filled with the Spirit until about three years ago (when she was forty-three years old). One precious thing I prayed for was the salvation of my household, consisting of:

Stanley Anderson, Sr.
Stanley Anderson, Jr.

George Franklin Anderson
Ellett Anderson (the author)
Jack Anderson
Myself.

It may be after my death, but it is a fact . . . I
have prayed for you *earnestly* and *tearfully* . . .
my prayers are bottled up (Rev. 5:8; 8:3-4). When
you give your hearts to Jesus, then seek the deep
spiritual life, the life directed by God. Don't fail
to study God's Word, for there is the secret. I expect
to see you, everyone, throughout the Blessed Eter-
nity with Jesus."

These words express the faith of Lillie Anderson.
Following a revival in the First Baptist Church of
Cheraw, at which time her two oldest children were
saved, Lillie decided to join the Baptist church with
her husband and sons. She, Stanley, Jr., and George
were the first three people to be baptized in the
new church building.

I came on the scene just before this event. I was
born on Sunday afternoon, June 5, 1927, the fifth
of mother's seven children. (Three died in infancy.)
I made a weighty entrance at twelve pounds and
was named Ellett Sherrill after my father's mother
(Mary Ellett) and my mother's people.

Great concern spread over the fact that I did
not begin talking when I should have. My first
complete sentence occurred when my Grand-
mother Sherrill tried to coax me into eating stewed
rabbit. I cried and said, "Me don't want no crooked
drumstick!" Of all things—my first sentence was
about food, and here I am writing about fasting!

Cheraw is a beautiful little town tucked away in the sandhills of northeast South Carolina. Few places are as beautiful in the springtime as this magnolia-tree-lined town. A blanket of azaleas and camellias of many hues covers the ground, shaded by white and pink dogwood trees, giving the entire area a fairyland appearance. Stately antebellum homes give dignity to the uptown and outlying areas, reminding residents and visitors alike of the town's rich history and heritage.

On the edge of town, near the muddy Pee Dee River, stands old St. David's Episcopal Church and cemetery. This lovely white frame building, still bearing the marks and bruises of cannonballs from the Revolutionary War, stands guard over hundreds of grave markers, many stained black with age. This little church was used as a hospital during the Revolutionary War, and many troops (British as well as American) were treated within its walls.

The first monument to Confederate soldiers who died during the brutal War Between the States was erected in this cemetery. As a young lad I joined in the procession each year on Memorial Day, when all the schoolchildren marched from the grammar school to St. David's, singing old war songs from the past and scattering wild flowers over the graves of those killed in action. It was meaningful to all of us and instilled in our minds an aversion to war and killing.

The First Baptist Church became a nest of burdened Christians—burdened for revival. Individuals from the other churches joined them in prayer. Home prayer meetings coupled with Bible classes sprang up all over the area. In 1938 the Christian Businessmen's Association formulated plans to construct a wooden "tabernacle" with a seating capacity of approximately a thousand people. The dirt floor was covered with wood shavings and sawdust, and the pews were the brush-arbor type—simple planks nailed together. Months of prayer and preparation preceded the coming of evangelist Jimmy Johnson of Fuquay Springs, North Carolina, and musician Joe Bamberg, now pastor of First Baptist Church, Milton, Florida (recently president of the Florida Baptist Convention).

Joe organized a "Booster Band" for the children, and we were rewarded for attending and for bringing others to the services. We learned choruses, Bible verses, and Bible stories. The stored-up prayers of the people of the community were unleashed. People attended by hundreds and, finally, thousands! This was amazing, as the population of the county was only between five thousand and seven thousand. People made decisions for Christ by the hundreds. In fact, during the month-long revival meeting, over one thousand made first-time decisions. Some people frown on this type of evangelism. And I suppose there are times when this is sham—but this one was genuine! I can recall several people whose lives were really changed.

My future wife (Eleanor) and I made peace with God during those wonderful days. (I was eleven years old, and she was ten.) Let me tell you what happened to me: One night I rode to the tabernacle with my mother and, I think, my three brothers.

We all went inside. I made my way to the Booster Band. There we sang our theme song:

> I belong to the Booster Band,
> I belong to the Booster Band!
> For God and right, I'll take my stand,
> I belong to the Booster Band.

(Isn't it amazing how we remember such things?) I remained in this particular area of the building even though some of the children returned to their parents when the regular service began. As the evangelist preached, I knew something was happening to me. I had never experienced it before. I felt I could not remain seated until he finished his sermon. But when he did and gave the invitation for those wishing to follow Jesus to come to the front of the building, I could not move. There was a force that seemed to hold me back.

Something about my reaction must have betrayed this indecision because a man right behind me placed his hand on my shoulder and asked, "Can I walk with you to the front?"

My courage took over, and I said, "No, sir, I can go by myself now." At the front, I shook hands with the evangelist, who instructed me to go into the prayer room. So many people were responding to the invitation each night that they needed a room for the inquirers to be counseled in. I do not recall seeing anyone else in the room as I entered. I simply knelt by myself.

Almost immediately I felt an arm around my shoulders and heard the soft weeping of a lady. I recognized the sobs; I had heard them before.

The lady was my mother. Upon arriving at the tabernacle that night, she had made her way into the prayer room. Instead of enjoying the great music and exciting preaching in the big tabernacle, she had spent more than an hour on her knees in this semidark side room, praying for her eleven-year-old son, who needed to be saved. That was the night I surrendered my heart, my mind, my will, my soul, and my life to Jesus Christ.

The kitchen in our home was quite large. One wall contained a double sink and over that was a cabinet containing cleaning products. Hanging from the lower right side of that cabinet was a water dipper. Whenever we wanted a drink of water, we drew it from the faucet and drank from the dipper. I remember, over the years, two of these dippers. The first was made of aluminum. The soft metal was soon bent from being dropped and bumped around so much. It was later replaced by a white enamel model that had a black rim around the top. It received the same rough treatment and soon became chipped and ugly.

This same wall also contained one of the pantries. Small jars of pickles, preserves, jellies, and so forth could be found there; and for some reason, a five-cent box of wooden matches was also kept there. In the corner near the door that led to the back porch was a skirted table with shelves underneath. On these shelves were cans of staples such as flour, lard, and the like. In the corner nearest the dining room was the stove. It was a six-eyed, coal-burning model. Mother knew just how to control the heat under each cooking surface. Next to the stove was the coal bin, where the fuel for the stove was kept. The fire seldom went out as it seemed that Mother was simmering something most of the time.

Somewhere around the stove could usually be found a bowl of milk that was clabbering to become the source of buttermilk. Above the stove were two compartments for keeping food warm. There we could always find some leftover biscuits. When I arrived home each afternoon from school, I would take a couple of these biscuits, punch holes in the top with my thumb, and fill the holes with molasses. This was a gourmet's delight!

In the center of the kitchen was the table, large enough for eight people to sit around. Ten could be seated if necessary. There was a chair at each end, three chairs on one side, and a long bench on the other side. Mother sat at one end; Dad was on her right. The older boys sat in the chairs, and the younger ones lined up on the bench. Some of my fondest memories took place at that spot. One of my earliest recollections is of sitting in a high chair between my parents during breakfast, while both of them fed me hot oatmeal. One could not spoon it up fast enough, so it took two! I still like oatmeal to this day . . . hmmmm. . .mm, good!

I remember wondering why my mother, at times, did not sit at the table and eat with us. Of course, most of the time she did. But once in a while it was obvious that something was going on that I did not understand. I do not recall that anyone ever asked her about it. Now, as I look back, I know she was fasting.

Each week Mother taught two Bible classes in our home. One of these was for adults and continues today in the home of one of her pupils. The other class was for children. I was a charter member of this one. How well I recall some of the Bible truths that I learned in these Bible classes. Mother, even then, was expecting the return of Jesus Christ any day! As an object lesson, she would spread various little items over a tabletop—things like tacks, buttons, pins, and marbles. "These things," she would say, "represent people—all kinds of people in the world." Then she would take a large magnet and bring it down close to the objects on the table. "This magnet represents Jesus," she would continue, "as he comes back to earth for his own."

As she brought the magnet closer and closer to the table, my heart would race. I watched the tacks, nails, and pins jump up and cling to the magnet before she raised it up high above her head and laid it on a shelf. I knew in my heart that it would be terrible to be left behind as were the buttons, marbles, and bits of paper remaining there on the table. I wanted to rush out on the streets and beg people to take Jesus into their hearts so that they would not be left here when he returns.

Even before Mother started these classes, she taught the Bible to my brothers and me. Before I entered the first grade, she saw that I "hid the Word in my heart" by memorizing over two hundred verses. I vaguely recall on several occasions that she commented on fasting in the Scriptures and shared some of her experiences. Because of my age, her words did not make much of an impression on me. My only thought at the time was that her goal must be important to cause her to miss that good food. Even until the day she died, I did not discuss fasting with her. I regret that now. It was my loss. I continued to try to live the Christian life without any real knowledge of the subject of fasting.

During my senior year in high school, I suffered a severe back injury while playing football. This resulted in fusion surgery and changed the course of my life. Earlier, I had experienced a definite call into full-time Christian ministry, although I did not know the specific field of service. Since church work was not my choice of a vocation, I pursued sports. Without this back injury, I would have continued to run from the Lord. However, while lying in bed for almost three months in a plaster cast from shoulders to hips, I decided to accept God's will for my life.

The most beautiful person I ever laid eyes on was a girl named Eleanor Haley. My heart beat faster every time I saw her with the sun shining on her long, thick auburn hair or smelled her perfume. Let me share how I was affected by her presence. While in high school I was employed in the meat department of a grocery store. One afternoon while I was at the hamburger grinder, she sort of floated into the store. I looked up and forgot what I was doing. Before I knew what was happening, I had ground off the end of a finger. On another occasion when she dropped by, I, unfortunately, was at the bacon slicer. I am afraid that one of the customers had more than bacon in his purchase. I had to get out of the meat business before I lost all ten fingers!

We were married very young, and I still feel that I was most fortunate when she became my bride. We have experienced a beautiful marriage relationship for over thirty years.

Shortly after our wedding we entered the Atlanta Bible Institute in Atlanta, Georgia. At the time I did not know the difference between a denominational school and an interdenominational one, and I had no guidance from anyone. Without a doubt, Eleanor and I felt that we were in God's will. We witnessed this evidence all around us. Not only was our knowledge of the Bible increased during these years, but some of our "rough edges" were knocked off. We learned to depend on God for our daily needs.

I recall the day when God supplied a ride from the school to downtown Atlanta. Eleanor and I were both employed in secular jobs while attending school. I had classes during the day and worked at night. She took night classes and worked during the day. On this particular day, we had no money at all. We had paid our tuition, room, and board, and our salaries were very small. Today was payday, but in the meantime there were over twenty blocks between school and Eleanor's job.

As we left the breakfast table in the dining hall that morning, Eleanor asked, "Honey, do you have a dime I could use for bus fare?" "I sure don't,"

I replied, emptying out my pockets. "Well," she said, "I guess I'll go on . . ." and left. I wondered if she planned to walk the twenty blocks . . . but no . . . she was walking toward the bus stop! Just then I spied another classmate nearby, and I ran toward him to see if I could borrow a dime for Eleanor.

At that a beautiful lady driving an expensive car pulled up to the bus stop and called out, "Young lady, do you need a ride to town?" I stood and watched, openmouthed, as my little wife waved to me and climbed into the Cadillac as if she had known all along it would be there! I hung my head, dropped my shoulders, and recrossed West Peachtree Street. But with every step my head rose a little and my shoulders straightened—my, what a God! We had thought in terms of a dime and God provided a Cadillac for Eleanor's ride to town. Several experiences like this helped to prepare us for what was yet to come. We learned much about prayer, but almost nothing about fasting—even though, like most college students, we did without meals several times along the way.

The week before graduation, I was called to pastor the West Bainbridge Baptist Church in Bainbridge, Georgia. I accepted their call and was ordained into the Southern Baptist ministry by the Northside Park Baptist Church in Atlanta, Georgia, where I had worked with the pastor, Ed McGee (now he is assistant pastor of Byne Memorial Baptist Church in Albany, Ga.). This man was most influential in my life, as he taught me how to witness to the unsaved and lead them to a personal faith in Jesus. I was also exposed to the deeper life as we worked together in evangelistic meetings. Through none of these great experiences was I exposed to fasting. God continued to use me and to bless my ministry. I want to say emphatically that fasting is *not* a prerequisite to being blessed and used by God. The Holy Spirit can definitely empower and use a person who does not fast.

The next time fasting crossed my path was in a revival meeting in a central Florida town. I was the guest evangelist of the First Baptist Church. The only other church in the area was the First Methodist Church, and the Methodist pastor attended the revival every night. He asked if I would consider preaching a series of sermons in his church. About two months later I did return and held a revival in his church.

One afternoon the Methodist pastor and I had been visiting in the community, and we drove by the parsonage to pick up his wife for supper. I sat in the living room while he went into the bedroom where he thought his wife was getting dressed. I overheard her say to him, "I can't go with you to supper this evening . . . I have been fasting all day. I feel like I will die unless God gives us a revival this time." We left without her. Needless to say, God blessed that church in an unusual way. But, like the "wayside" heart in the parable of the sower (Matt. 13:1-8), the "fowls of the air" came and "devoured" the impact of this event from me.

I did not experience another fasting event for years.

Even as I continued my education in Luther Rice

Seminary, Jacksonville, Florida, completing my Master of Theology degree and working toward my Doctor of Ministries, I had no fasting experience. One New Testament verse, however, continued to press upon me. On the day of the transfiguration, when Jesus, Peter, James, and John descended from the mountain, they were approached by a man with his demon-possessed child. The disciples, who had not been permitted to climb the mount with Jesus, had been unable to cast out the evil spirit. After Jesus performed the healing miracle, he answered his disciples' question, "Why could not we cast him out?" by saying, "This kind can come forth by nothing, but by prayer and fasting" (Mark 9:28-29). This time the seed would find the fertile soil in my heart.

For twenty-six years I preached the gospel of Jesus Christ. God blessed it by adding to the church an average of over one hundred baptisms plus one hundred other additions per year. I guess I was satisfied to have this measure of success. During my sixteenth year as pastor of the Riverside Baptist Church, Fort Myers, Florida, the matter of fasting became an obsession. This was encouraged when the minister of youth, Larry Ferguson, encouraged our young people to set aside one day each week and fast for revival.

My youngest daughter, Sonja, selected Sunday as her special day. Sunday happened to be the day when our family got together for dinner. Eleanor and I are proud of our family. Our oldest daughter, Mary Anne, her husband, Dale Conn, and their three children; along with our son, Ron, his wife,

Nancy, and their daughter; Sonja, her husband, Dwight Locke, and Eleanor and I eat together on Sunday. Obviously, this is one of the most meaningful days of the week for us.

At that time, as we ate together, Sonja drank only a glass of iced tea. No one knows how this affected me, for I had a guilty conscience already. I had observed a marked change in the lives of our church youth, and especially I noted the inner joy that Sonja experienced. These observations weighed heavily on my mind. It seemed as if God were working me into a corner where I would be forced to act.

On top of all this, our church ceased to grow. In the twenty-six years of my pastorates, I had never experienced this situation. It seemed that nothing I did reversed this downward trend. During this growthless period the word *fast* continued to press upon me. Finally I decided to act—I would fast!

When this decision was made, I realized how little I knew about the subject. I began to look around for someone who practiced fasting as a way of life. I found no one. I tried to find a book on the subject, but my search was futile. I then returned to the Book, where I should have started at first. I read the Bible through, noting the places where fasting is mentioned. I found an abundance of facts that had gone unnoticed in my previous studies.

There seemed to be a whole dimension of the Christian experience that I had never discovered.

2 Fasting and Medical Science

I wanted to know what medical science said about fasting. Obviously, I did not want to injure my body; and, if possible, I wanted to know what physical reactions I would experience. I have found very few doctors who know anything about the subject and fewer who have practiced it. But I include in this chapter the information I have found.

My study of fasting is primarily a search into the spiritual implications; therefore, this medical chapter is brief. I want it clearly understood that *I am not recommending fasting as a cure of disease.* I am not a doctor. Often I am asked, "Will fasting cure high blood pressure?" or "Will fasting help my arthritis?" or other questions of this nature. This chapter does not teach fasting as a cure. However, since fasting slows us down, helps us lose weight, and harmonizes the relationship with God and man, some physical and emotional benefits are bound to result.

Fasting Is Not Starving

God is a wonderful Designer. He made the body to be a storehouse. Knowing that man could not eat on exact schedules, he made the body so that the muscles, tissues, and blood could store the nutrients. As long as food is available, the body uses what it needs and conserves the remainder. When food is not available, the body absorbs these reserves. Obviously, when the reserves are exhausted, starvation begins. But also in God's omniscience, he established a mechanism which protects the vital parts of the body until all else is consumed. Although I have not experienced an ultimate fast, I am told that a person knows when the natural end of the fast has been reached.

Arthur Blessitt (whose testimony is found later in this book) and his wife experienced a forty-day fast while in Washington, DC. When talking with him I asked, "How long can a person safely fast?" Arthur is a minister of the gospel and not a doctor, but his answer was, "I don't know, Andy, but if the Lord burdens a person with a forty-day fast, a person can do it with no harm done to his body. There are medically-induced fasts which are much longer—over 100 days, I understand, but I've had no experience with them. The longest fast in the Bible was a forty-day fast, so I know it's safe."

Certainly no one should go on a lengthy fast without medical supervision. Common sense indicates that the body cannot exist indefinitely without nutrition. Common abstinence from food is necessary in some digestive troubles in order to give the stomach and intestinal tract a chance to get well. In cases of high fever, when the digestive juices and ferments are produced in small amounts or not at all, no food may be given for a limited time.

The Irishman MacSwinney starved to death in prison while fasting for political reasons after more than fifty days without food. Research has shown that, after fasting, metabolism can become as much as 22 percent lower than the normal rate. But it has also been found that, after periods of long fasting, the body tends to adjust itself by lowering the rate of metabolism. The body has many reserves when attacked by hunger. Stored animal starch (glycogen) and fat feed the body for a time. Muscle and other protein tissues supply heat and energy when these reserves are exhausted.

These and other facts indicate that lengthy fasts to starve oneself are dangerous unless done under the care of a physician. But the observance of fasting as practiced by Christians will promote self-control and strengthen the will.

Will Fasting Cure Disease?

Throughout history medical quacks have claimed that fasting will cure everything from freckles to falling arches. But the medical literature I have studied does not so indicate.

As I travel throughout America I sometimes speak on this subject. Almost without exception several people come to the front of the auditorium to discuss the subject. Some of them have fasted and want to share their experiences. Others want to discuss some specific facet of fasting and still others want to ask questions. Very few have done any research but have heard some "old wive's fables" and want to check them out.

At Rock Eagle encampment in Georgia a lady

said she understood that almost every disease could be cured by fasting. I answered that I found no evidence to substantiate that. But, I continued, it is obvious that bad physical condition brought on by overweight can be helped by weight loss. I mentioned that high blood pressure could be reduced and cholesterol levels would go down if there were significant loss of weight. Some doctors are experimenting with fasts to help schizophrenic patients. I heard that one doctor reports up to 70 percent of his patients being restored to active life through fasting. When a person goes on a fast, the digestive system gets a rest. No longer is there an overstuffed feeling. The stomach and intestines empty. The body feels clean and lean. Much of the energy which has been used in digestion is then available for other things.

Some doctors agree that planned fasts are very beneficial for bodily health, whereas others disagree by saying it produces a "stress situation."

Dr. Allan Cott, author of *Fasting: The Ultimate Diet,* believes that fasting, far from being a stress situation, is a means of providing "welcome rest for the digestive tract and central nervous system. It normalizes metabolism. The kidney preserves potassium and sugar in the blood—an important element that assures our feeling of well-being."[1]

Without exception, every practicing faster I have interviewed has expressed a heightened state of consciousness following a three-day or more fast. This has also been my experience. Blessitt was the first person who mentioned this to me. This does not seem to be experienced until after the third or fourth day, however. The mind becomes extremely sharp, thoughts exceptionally clear.

Not long ago I spoke on Fasting in Bristol, Virginia. A man commented afterward that he didn't believe he could fast because it would make him weak, and his job required strength. Now I'm sure that a person's physical condition would make a difference but I personally do not undergo this weakness. I carry on my activities as if I were consuming a T-bone steak nightly. It is general knowledge that Dick Gregory ran in the Boston Marathon during a lengthy fast.

I suppose the most often-asked question is, "Does fasting produce any unpleasant side effects?"

I have found only three unpleasant, but not unbearable, physical effects: (1) a lightness in my head, (2) a bad taste in my mouth, and (3) foul breath. These three are experienced by almost all people who fast three or more days. Since few people fast that long, these would not be a problem. However, I detect my lightness of head more during the second day than at any other time. After the third day it seems that some fasters experience other side effects. Headache, dizziness, lower back pain are a few; however, none of the people I have interviewed have had these problems.

Dr. Otto H. F. Buchinger, who has supervised more than seventy thousand fasts, writes, "Fasting is . . . a royal road to healing for anyone who agrees to take it for the recovery and regeneration of the body, mind and spirit."[2]

Health Pluses

In Chapter 7, "Benefits of Fasting," I will give details about the spiritual and emotional pluses of fasting. Here let me sum up the medical and health factors.

Controlled fasting will help the body purge itself of toxic substances. Fasting can cleanse the system as your intake consists of water only.

People who begin to fast often report that, after the fast, their energy is far greater. They often sleep better without tumbling or tossing. They may wake up more refreshed, rather than feeling dead tired at the beginning of the day. They seem calmer and less frustrated, in spite of the pressures on them. They are proud because of the pounds they have lost. They feel a new sense of mastery and self-confidence, even though the fast may have lasted no more than three to five days.

They report that fasting can lead to increased energy, calmness, better attention to the work at hand, and good feelings about oneself.

There are those who start to fast because of sickness, of course. Some, though, to improve health that is already good. The person who fasts also begins to look at life differently. Even though he may be involved in pressure-packed activity, the pace does not seem as frenetic. He tends to look at the world through less jaundiced, less dissipated eyes.

Many fasters say that fasting helps them to control runaway emotions. There seems to be more understanding and less uptightness.

Fasters of many persuasions have used fasting

to detach themselves from worry and anxiety. One's health is better through *discipline,* as much as people hate that word today. We are living in an eat-drink-be merry society. Christianity, and any great system of thought, stress control of one's passions and appetites. For the moment that may not sound like good advice, but it begins to make sense later in life as a person breaks down because of earlier neglect.

Those who emphasize fasting like to view the human being as a mental, physical, and spiritual entity. They believe that an ill body can recuperate through proper fasting. The body can repair itself through fasting.

The traditional definition of fasting has been: "To abstain from food as a religious observance." In the broadest sense, that is no longer true. Fasting may have religious or non-religious reasons. Thousands are fasting for the sake of their health and with no religious intent. Others fast for religious reasons only. Many others combine the religious and health motives, probably the best possible approach.

Medical science, religion, and philosophy have clearly shown the benefits of fasting.

3 Fasting and the Bible

Fasting is found seventy-five times in the Scriptures, forty-four times in the Old Testament and thirty-one times in the New Testament.

In the Hebrew language of the Old Testament it is pronounced *tsoon* and means to cover the mouth, to fast. In the Greek language of the New Testament it is pronounced *nacetis* and means to not eat, to abstain from food, to fast.

It is interesting that this word is not found in the Gospel of John, although it is found in the other three Gospels. It is not found in the apostle Paul's theology, although there is much evidence that he practiced it.

It is also interesting to note that the Bible does not tell us *how* to fast, *how often* to fast, or *how long* to fast. Some religious leaders teach or suggest that one day a week should be set aside for fasting. Many have found this practice beneficial; however, it is not suggested in the Bible.

The Most Complete Chapter on Fasting

The fifty-eighth chapter of Isaiah contains the Bible's most complete account of fasting. These first fourteen verses should be thoroughly digested by everyone who is interested in knowing the mind of God concerning the subject. An outline for your study may be:

Man's question to God, "Why have you not honored our fasts?" (vv. 1-3)

God's answer to man, "Your life contradicts your fast" (vv. 3-5)

God's question to man, "Is this the kind of fast I desire?" (v. 5)

God's answer to his own question, "My kind of fast produces genuine godliness and immense blessings" (vv. 6-14).

Let us examine this chapter a little more closely while following the above outline.

Man asks God, "Why have you not honored our fasts? Why have we fasted and thou not seen? Why have we humbled ourselves and thou not noticed?" As we continue to read the text we note that their action was hypocritical and insincere. Religious activity can easily become meaningless even as the fast became meaningless in the lives of the Pharisees in the New Testament. Christian service must be guarded with prayer. "Is there any greater blindness than religious self-deception?" (James Lee Beall).

God answers with a fourfold reprimand: (1) Your time of the fast is a time of pleasure rather than mourning; (2) you do not change your attitude toward your slaves; you drive them hard; (3) your attitude is wrong; you are filled with contention and strife; (4) you are selfish, striking with a wicked fist.

The blame is not to be placed on God. The fast-er cannot be blessed because of his unwillingness to confess his sins and turn from them. These sins are in the form of both attitude and activity. The psalmist said, "If I regard iniquity in my heart, the Lord will not hear me" (Ps. 66:18).

God now poses the question to man, "Is this the kind of fast I desire? Do you think that it is enough just to humble yourself or bow like a reed in the wind or make a bed of sackcloth and ashes? Do you call that an acceptable fast?"

"No," God answers. "My kind of fast is the kind which produces the:

—loosing of the bonds of wickedness (v. 6)
—undoing of the bands of the yoke (v. 6), breaking of every yoke (v. 6), and removing of the yoke from your midst (v. 9)
—allowing of the oppressed to go free (v. 6)
—dividing of bread (food) with the hungry, bringing of the homeless into your home (shelter), and covering (clothing) of the naked (v. 7)
—hiding not from family needs (v. 7)
—ceasing of the pointing of your finger (v. 9)
—stopping of the speaking of wickedness (v. 9)
—giving of yourself to the hungry (v. 10)
—satisfying of the desire of the afflicted (v. 10)
—honoring of the Lord's Day (v. 13).

Now God states the benefits that come to those who practice his kind of fast. It is almost impossible to belive what he says. Read the list slowly and determine that these benefits will be yours. The

Lord says, *I will:*

—allow light to break out like the dawn (vv. 8,10)
—allow recovery to speedily spring forth (vv. 8, 11)
—allow righteousness to go before you and his glory to go behind you (vv. 8,11)
—allow your calls and cries to be heard (v. 9)
—allow light to rise in darkness (v. 10)
—allow the gloom to become like midday (v. 10)
—continually guide you (v. 11)
—satisfy your desire in the scorched place (v. 11)
—give strength to your bones (v. 11)
—allow you to be like a watered garden and like a spring that does not lose its water (v. 11)
—see that from among you will come those who will rebuild ancient ruins, raise up old foundations, be called the repairer of the breach, and be called the restorer of the streets in which to live (v. 12)
—allow you to delight in the Lord, to ride the heights of the earth, to be fed with the heritage of Jacob (v. 14)
—allow you the privilege of finding assurance in God's word (v. 14).

This is one of the most astounding chapters in the Bible. Many Christians are seeking the abundant life spoken of in these promises. God says that the right kind of fast produces it.

Two men were discussing this subject with me one evening, and one surprised me by saying, "Andy, I've fasted on several occasions; and nothing happened. I just got hungry."

I asked him to share his experiences. "Well,"

he continued, several years ago I heard a couple of pastors discussing fasting. On their recommendation I tried my first fast. They said it was commanded in the Bible and should be practiced by every Christian. Being a Christian, I decided to try it. After putting it off for several days, I mustered up enough courage to start. I couldn't go to the breakfast table with my family because I didn't think I would have enough willpower to abstain from eating, so I went on to work. The coffee break was almost unbearable, and I told a little white lie about why I didn't go with the group. All I could think about was how hungry I was. I said to myself, *If I ever get through this day, I'll never try this again.*

"The afternoon was even worse. I tried to concentrate on my work, but all I could hear was the growling of my stomach. My wife prepared a meal for herself and our child, and the aroma of the food was all I could bear. I figured that if I could make it till midnight, I would have fasted all day. I did—but immediately after the striking of the hour of twelve, I dug into food. I don't think that day of fasting helped me one bit."

Neither time nor space will permit me to record our two-hour conversation, but let us examine this man's fast.

First, God obviously had not burdened this Christian to fast. His motive had no conviction—only what someone else had said. Then, the purpose of the fast was only to endure twelve hours without food. All he concentrated on was his hunger. There was no evidence that he mourned over his sins or sought the will of God. This was only a no-food diet (he admitted he lost one pound). It was not a biblical fast.

Later in the conversation the real problem surfaced. He admitted a serious problem between himself and another church member. While he was fasting he was doubly irritable and ill tempered. God says, "What good is fasting when you keep on fighting and quarreling?"

One of the major reasons for the fast is the examining of the heart, admitting personality problems, and straightening them out. It was easy to see why nothing happened in this man's life. He missed the entire point of the fast. No one can become involved with other people until he has been freed from selfishness. This is the area that makes fasting psychologically healthy and sound. It is the shifting of attention and care from yourself to others. Religious focus can easily turn inward. Regrettably, this inward turn happens to many. This is especially true for those who inordinately desire to be used by the Lord. They reason, "Perhaps if I fasted I could obtain more power, do more things, see more results, and be known by more people." This sounds good and extremely religious, but it is the wrong focus. The weight of attention is on what you will become. Amen and amen. The fast is not for the benefit of the fast-er.

The fast that God has chosen is to enable us to root out selfishness, which destroys our effectiveness with God and man. As we receive inner liberation from self and sin, we can help others. A few minutes each day should be spent in repenting of the sin of selfishness.

During my fasts I concentrate on the sins of my life. How hard it is to be totally honest with oneself! One by one these sins must be recalled and discussed with my Cleanser. "Doesn't that make you morbid?" I was asked. "It surely does, but not half as morbid as it must make God when I don't search them out."

I discover that I have a tendency to tuck away the "little sins" into the folds of my heart while I confess the "big sins." Therefore, the "biggies" do not give me as much trouble as the little ones. Selfishness is revealed through unconfessed sins. The fast is a time of digging them out. God's test is not easy to pass. It goes against the grain. It demands more than the natural man will give. It requires more than lip service. God's fast puts God's love into operation. Caring inevitably leads to sharing at the cost of inconvenience. It attests to our willingness for such sacrifices. Caring cannot stop with our words, not even religious words. Caring must be demonstrated.

Did not James state it in his writing? "If a brother or sister be naked, and destitute of daily food, And one of you say unto them, Depart in peace, be ye warmed and filled; notwithstanding ye give them not those things which are needful to the body; what doth it profit?" (2:15-16).

Fasting prepares us for sacrificial giving because we first gain the discipline of self-denial. We get our minds off ourselves and reorder our priorities. We become able to see our brother's need. Sharing is a spontaneous outflow of mercy when we have identified ourselves as on the same level as our brother. Humbling ourselves through fasting is a sure way to recognize how human we are.

Who Fasted in the Bible?

As I mentioned in the opening paragraph of this book, this is not a complete biblical study of the subject of fasting. However, I will lift from the Scriptures some of the most interesting and helpful verses. Here is a partial study of those who fasted:

Moses

"And the Lord said unto Moses, 'Write thou these words: for after the tenor of these words I have made a covenant with thee and with Israel.' And he was there with the Lord forty days and forty nights; he did neither eat bread, nor drink water. And he wrote upon the tables the words of the covenant, the ten commandments" (Ex. 34:27-28).

The Israelites

"Then all the children of Israel, and all the people, went up, and came unto the house of God, and wept, and sat there before the Lord, and fasted that day until even, and offered burnt offerings and peace offerings before the Lord" (Judg. 20:26).

The Jewish people were commanded to fast one day a year. "And this shall be a statute for ever unto you: that in the seventh month, on the tenth day of the month, ye shall afflict your souls (fast), and do not work at all" (Lev. 16:29).

Samuel

"And Samuel said, Gather all Israel to Mizpeh,
and I will pray for you unto the Lord. And they
gathered together to Mizpeh, and drew water, and
poured it out before the Lord, and fasted on that
day, and said there, We have sinned against the
Lord" (1 Sam. 7:5-6).

David

"Then David took hold on his clothes, and rent
them; and likewise all the men that were with him:
And they mourned, and wept, and fasted until even,
for Saul, and for Jonathan his son, . . . and for
the house of Israel; because they were fallen by
the sword" (2 Sam. 1:11-12).

Elijah

"Then Jezebel sent a messenger unto Elijah,
saying, So let the gods do to me, and mine also,
if I make not thy life as the life of one of them
by to morrow about this time. And he (Elijah) arose
and did eat and drink, and went in the strength
of that meat forty days and forty nights unto Horeb
the mount of God" (1 Kings 19:2,8).

Nehemiah

"And it came to pass, when I heard these words,
that I sat down and wept, and mourned certain
days, and fasted, and prayed before the God of
heaven" (Neh. 1:4).

Daniel

"And I set my face unto the Lord God, to seek by prayer and supplications, with fasting, and sackcloth, and ashes: And I prayed unto the Lord my God, and made my confession" (Dan. 9:3-4).

Anna

"And there was one Anna, a prophetess, the daughter of Phanuel, of the tribe of Aser: she was of a great age, and had lived with a husband seven years from her virginity; And she was a widow of about fourscore and four years, which departed not from the temple, but served God with fastings and prayers night and day" (Luke 2:36-37).

The Disciples of Jesus and John

"Moreover when ye fast, be not as the hypocrites, of a sad countenance" (Matt. 6:16).

"Jesus said unto them, Can the children of the bridechamber mourn, as long as the bridegroom is with them? but the days will come, when the bridegroom shall be taken from them, and then shall they fast" (Matt. 9:15).

"Then came to him the disciples of John, saying, Why do we and the Pharisees fast oft, but thy disciples fast not? " (Matt. 9:14).

Jesus

"then was Jesus led up of the spirit into the wilderness to be tempted of the devil. And when he had fasted forty days and forty nights, he was afterward an hungered" (Matt. 4:1-2).

Paul

"And when they had ordained them elders in every church, and had prayed with fasting, they commended them to the Lord, on whom they believed" (Acts 14:23).

Ninevites

"So the people of Nineveh believed God, and proclaimed a fast, and put on sackcloth, from the greatest of them even to the least of them" (Jonah 3:5).

"Then the king went to his palace, and passed the night fasting" (Dan. 6:18).

Pharisees

"I fast twice in the week" (Luke 18:12).

Cornelius

"And Cornelius said, Four days ago I was fasting until this hour; and at the ninth hour I prayed in my house, and, behold, a man stood before me in bright clothing" (Acts 10:30).

Sailors

"And while the day was coming on, Paul besought them all to take meat, saying, This day is the fourteenth day that ye have tarried and continued fasting, having taken nothing" (Acts 27:33).

I glean from this brief study several important facts:

1. Fasting does not produce a redemptive expe-

rience in the individual.

2. Fasting is not a way to reach God. Jesus said, "I am the way."

3. Fasting can be practiced by Christians and non-Christians.

4. Fasting may be only a formality.

5. In spite of the minuses, fasting can be a meaningful experience.

Under What Circumstances Did They Fast?

Described next are some of the circumstances under which fasting was practiced.

In Time of Defeat

"Then all the children of Israel, and all the people, went up, and came unto the house of God, and wept, and sat there before the Lord, and fasted that day until even, and offered burnt offerings and peace offerings before the Lord" (Judg. 20:26).

In Time of Repentance

"And they gathered together to Mizpeh, and drew water, and poured it out before the Lord and fasted on that day, and said there, 'We have sinned against the Lord' " (1 Sam. 7:6).

In Times of Discerning God's Will and Ordination

"As they ministered to the Lord, and fasted, the Holy Ghost said, Separate me Barnabas and Saul for the work whereunto I have called them. And when they had fasted and prayed, and laid their hands on them, they sent them away" (Acts 13:2-3).

In Time of Sorrow

"And they took their bones, and buried them under a tree at Jabesh, and fasted seven days" (1 Sam. 31:13).

In Time of Sickness

"Then said his servants unto him, What thing is this that thou hast done? Thou didst fast and weep for the child, while it was alive; but when the child was dead, thou didst rise and eat bread. And he said, While the child was yet alive, I fasted and wept: for I said, Who can tell whether God will be gracious to me, that the child may live?" (2 Sam. 12:21-22).

In Time of Death

"And they mourned, and wept, and fasted until even, for Saul, and for Jonathan his son, and for the people of the Lord, and for the house of Israel, because they were fallen by the sword" (2 Sam. 1:12).

In Time of Great Temptation

"Then was Jesus led up of the spirit into the wilderness to be tempted of the devil. And when he had fasted forty days and forty nights, he was afterward an hungered. And when the tempter came to him, he said, If thou be the Son of God, command that these stones be made bread. But he answered and said, It is written, Man shall not live by bread alone, but by every word that proceedeth out of the mouth of God" (Matt. 4:1-4).

These biblical events tell us that we should fast

when faced with similar situations.

What Were Some of the Lengths of Fasts?

Short Periods

"Defraud ye not one the other, except it be with consent for a time, that ye may give yourselves to fasting and prayer; and come together again, that Satan tempt your incontinency" (1 Cor. 7:5).

One Day

"Then all the children of Israel, and all the people went up, and came unto the house of God, and wept, and sat there before the Lord, and fasted that day until even" (Judg. 20:26).

Twice a Week

"I fast twice in the week" (Luke 18:12).

Seven Days

"And they took their bones, and buried them under a tree at Jabesh, and fasted seven days" (1 Sam. 31:13).

Fourteen Days

"And while the day was coming on, Paul besought them all to take meat, saying, This day is the fourteenth day that ye have tarried and continued fasting" (Acts 27:33).

Forty Days

REGULAR FORTY-DAY FAST

"And when he had fasted forty days and forty

nights, he was afterwards an hungered" (Matt. 4:2).
SUPERNATURAL FORTY-DAY FAST

"And he was there with the Lord forty days and
forty nights; he did neither eat bread, nor drink
water" (Ex. 34:28). God had to intervene because
a person cannot fast forty days without drinking
fluids. These events indicate that there is no established length of time for a fast. The Christian
should be willing to fast until God has completed
his purpose for the fast.

What Did Biblical Fasts Produce?

Frustration

In Isaiah 58:3 the people asked, "Wherefore have
we fasted . . . and thou seest not? wherefore have
we afflicted our soul, and thou takest no knowledge? " The motivation and purpose of this fast
were wrong.

Hunger

Luke 4:1-2 says, "And Jesus being full of the
Holy Ghost returned from Jordan, and was led by
the Spirit into the wilderness, Being forty days
tempted of the devil. And in those days he did
eat nothing: and when they were ended, he afterward hungered."

Victory

Matthew 4:2b-4 reads "He was afterward an
hungered. And when the tempter came to him, he
said, If thou be the Son of God, command that
these stones be made bread. But he answered and

said, It is written, Man shall not live by bread alone, but by every word that proceedeth out of the mouth of God."

The Presence of the Supernatural

This truth is vividly described in Matthew 4:2-4, 11. Note that the devil came to tempt Jesus. Verse 11 says, "The devil leaveth him, and behold, angels came and ministered unto him." When Jesus fasted, he discovered that both supernatural powers were present—the devil and the angels of God.

In my own experience with fasting, this has been true—the only time in my travels I have been approached by prostitutes have been times of fasting. It is as if the devil were present to tempt. But let me hasten to say that these temptations were not hard to resist because I had an awesome sense of the presence of God with me.

I once flew from my hometown, Fort Myers, Florida, to Atlanta, Georgia. From there I went to St. Louis, Missouri and on to Portland, Oregon. The day before I left Florida, January 1, 1976, I was impressed that I should begin the New Year with a fast. My diary reads, "I did not eat as I traveled by plane from the extreme southeastern state to the extreme northwestern state in the United States. I drank much water, however. I carried my New Testament in my attaché case and read from it throughout the day. I probably looked to my fellow passengers as if I were asleep, but my heart was being lifted to God in prayer. I zeroed in on the sins in my life."

Now, I always confess my sins—that is, those

I hurriedly remember; but on that day, I had looked
for the little things I had tried to hide from God.
None of these seemed important, but I knew I had
not confessed them. I had tucked them away in
the folds of my heart. My prayer was that God
would help me to remember them, and he did.
As the thousands of miles passed beneath the wings
of the plane and as the hours ticked away on the
clock, I could almost feel the weight of these sins
lifting from me. I am not an overly emotional
person, but I felt like laughing and crying and
singing all at the same time. But if you do that
on a plane, you will receive some funny glances.

I knew that the purpose of this fast was being
achieved. God was cleansing my life and filling
me with an inner peace I had known but few times
before. Upon my arrival in Portland my host delivered me to the motel so that I could rest for a
while, shower, and dress for the evening meeting.
Shortly after I lay down, the telephone rang.

"Mr. Anderson?" a female voice asked.

"Yes, this is he," I replied.

"I'm checking to see if your room is satisfactory."

"Yes, it is—it is quite adequate."

"Is there anything you need?"

At this point I began to wonder. I have found
employees at motels very friendly, but this was
one step too far.

She continued, "We can supply whatever service
you desire."

I knew then that a prostitute was making a pitch.
I did not know how she got my name and room
number, but obviously she had. "No, I do not desire

anything. I am here as guest minister at the
_____ Baptist Church."

"We are glad to have you in our city."

At this point, she hung up the phone.

God being my witness, though Satan had stepped
into my life through this woman, the angels of God
ministered to me. There was no real decision for
me to make; the temptation simply disappeared.
At the church that night "heaven came down," and
God's Spirit led us through an exciting spiritual
experience.

Back at the motel, I knelt by the bed to thank
the Lord for what had taken place at the church.
The telephone conversation of a few hours earlier
was totally forgotten when I heard a knock at my
door. I thought it was my host returning to tell
me something—but it wasn't. Few people are more
careful than I am when in a motel room. I always
lock and chain the door as soon as I enter the room.
I cracked the door as far as the chain would allow,
only to see an attractive woman very suggestively
dressed. There was no doubt who she was or what
her purpose was. I closed the door with an emphatic
_No!_ I again fell to my knees and prayed.

I repeat the earlier paragraph. God being my
witness, though Satan stepped into my life through
this woman, the angels of God ministered to me.
There was no real decision for me to make; the
temptation simply disappeared. Before I arose from
my knees, I prayed for that woman. I prayed that
somewhere, someone could tell her the story of
Jesus, who could forgive her as he had the prostitute
in the New Testament. This illustrates that during

fasts I have experienced satanic temptations, but also the presence of God—both supernatural powers. But God is superior to Satan.

God's Will in Ordination

One of my greatest concerns over the last thirty years has been the large number of ordained men who drop out of the ministry. If God called them and separated them to his ministry, what happened? After interviewing many of these good men—men of God—I have discovered that a mistake was made in ordaining some of them. Sometimes the fault was the man's. Under emotional circumstances or pressures, he allowed a church to ordain him. Sometimes the responsibility lay with an overzealous pastor or church. These mistakes leave a person frustrated. Often ordained men try to continue in a particular ministry, even if they know they are out of God's will. Social and religious pressures prevent them from saying, "I made a mistake."

Only after I began studying the subject of fasting did I see the following truth. Acts 13:1-3 says, "Now there were in the church that was at Antioch certain prophets and teachers; as Barnabas, and Simeon that was called Niger, and Lucius of Cyrene, and Manaen, which had been brought up with Herod the tetrarch, and Saul. As they ministered to the Lord, and fasted, the Holy Ghost said, Separate me Barnabas and Saul for the work whereunto I have called them. And when they had fasted and prayed, and laid their hands on them, they sent them away."

Here are two fasts. The first took place before God revealed to the church that these two laymen were called for specific service. The second took place before their ordination. Perhaps the church and candidates would make fewer mistakes in this matter if it were resolved through fasting before ordination.

Later, in the life of the church, the apostle Paul visited many cities; among these were Lystra, Iconium, and Antioch. "And when they had ordained them elders in every church, and had prayed with fasting, they commended them to the Lord, on whom they believed" (Acts 14:23).

Obviously fasting at the time of ordination was a practice of the New Testament church.

A Service for God

An elderly widow used fasting as a method of serving God. "And there was one Anna, a prophetess, the daughter of Phanuel, of the tribe of Aser: she was of great age, and had lived with an husband seven years from her virginity; And she was a widow of about fourscore and four years, which departed not from the temple, but served God with fastings and prayers night and day" (Luke 2:36-37). This is a service that has been overlooked today.

Paul spoke of ministering to God by fasting. "But in all things approving ourselves as the ministers of God, in much patience, in afflictions, in necessities, in distresses, In stripes, in labours, in watchings, in fastings . . ." (2 Cor. 6:4-5).

Special Power for Difficult Miracles

Perhaps the most often quoted verses in the Bible relating to fasting are found in Matthew 17:18-21. "And Jesus rebuked the devil; and he (the unclean spirit) departed out of him: and the child was cured from that very hour. Then came the disciples to Jesus apart, and said, Why could we not cast him out? And Jesus said unto them, Because of your unbelief: for verily I say unto you, If ye have faith as a grain of mustard seed, ye shall say unto this mountain, Remove hence to yonder place; and it shall remove; and nothing shall be impossible unto you. Howbeit this kind goeth not out but by prayer and fasting."

Some people think this story teaches that if you cannot get God to act after you pray, you can couple fasting with prayer and twist the arm of God. No one twists the arm of God.

What the verses really say is that if a person has emptied himself of sin and is in proper relationship with God, the difficult miracles will be performed. The psalmist said, "If I regard iniquity in my heart, the Lord will not hear me" (Ps. 66:18).

A Vision

There are conflicting opinions concerning people's experiencing visions. The purpose of this book is not to try to solve this debate but to state what took place in a biblical account. In Acts 10 we have the fascinating account of how a non-Christian seeker found God. In the thirtieth and thirty-first verses, "Cornelius said, Four days ago I was fasting until this hour; and at the ninth hour I prayed in my house, and, behold, a man stood before me in bright clothing, And said, Cornelius, thy prayer is heard, and thine alms are had in remembrance in the sight of God."

In response to the fasting and prayer of a non-Christian, God revealed himself to Cornelius.

The Will of God

In Judges we read the story of a great war. The people of God, Israel, had sinned greatly and had lost the battle—eighteen thousand soldiers were slain. In order to discover the will of God as to what they were to do, "Then all the children of Israel, and all the people, went up, and came unto the house of God, and wept, and sat there before' the Lord, and fasted that day until even, and offered burnt offerings and peace offerings before the Lord" (Judg. 20:26).

4 Fasting and the Spiritual Life

There is a major emphasis today on the deeper, Spirit-filled life. A large part of the thrust is on the receiving of the gifts of the Spirit. Camps and retreats are conducted to promote it; new books on the subject are rolling from the presses; sermons thunder forth from pulpit, radio and television on this important subject as if it were just discovered. But there can be no deeper or Spirit-filled life until there is a thorough repenting from and cleansing of sin. Very little emphasis is placed on this subject.

This is where the biblical fast comes into focus. It is a time when the seeker after God becomes earnest enough to pay the price for cleanliness. It is impossible to have fellowship with God on our easy terms. Our idea of repentance is to spend fifteen minutes in Bible study followed by a prayer for God to "forgive me of all my sins." But biblical accounts portray men and women fasting in sack-cloth and ashes for days and weeks while waiting upon God to finish his perfect work.

Some have never learned the indissoluble marriage of religion and ethics; they are seeking a divorce between them. They have a thoroughly inadequate doctrine of sin and its sinfulness in relation to the Holy God. Christianity is the only religion that by emphasizing that God is holy, first insists on taking sin seriously and then offers a forgiveness. The way to have fellowship with the holy God is not to deny the fact of the effects of sin, but to confess them and receive his forgiveness.

There is a thorough discussion of this matter in 1 John 1. In verse 6 there is a false claim that a person can have fellowship with God while habitually walking in darkness, sin. This is the person who claims he can be righteous without doing right. Religion without morality is an illusion. If we claim we are right with God and yet habitually live in sin, "we lie."

"Walking in the light" describes absolute sincerity with no attempt to conceal anything from God. Only when this is accomplished is there any hope for intimate fellowship with God. When we are "walking in the light," God provides even another blessing—"the blood of Jesus Christ his Son cleanseth us from all sin" (1 John 1:7). This suggests that God does more than forgive, he erases the stain of sin. The tense of the Greek verb shows that it is a continuous process.

If we walk in the light, God has made provision to cleanse us from whatever sin would mar our fellowship with him or each other.

There is a second erroneous claim in John's epistle which is worse than the first. The first heretical claim at least concedes the existence of sin. The second claim is to "have no sin"—to be sinless. These deny the very fact of sin. Now, to say we have no sin means that "we deceive ourselves"— that is, we are self-deceived rather than deliberate

liars. This teaching is applicable today to those who
deny the fact or guilt of sin by seeking to interpret
it solely in terms of psychological, social, or physi-
ological causes. The proper attitude toward sin is
not to deny it but to admit it and to confess it
so as to receive forgiveness.

"If we confess our sins," acknowledge them before God, he will both "forgive us and cleanse us
from all unrighteousness." He is "faithful" to forgive because he has promised to do so, and "just"
because Jesus died for our sins. This, however, is
conditioned upon our confession.

The most blatant of the claims is the third one.
The heretics maintain that their superior knowledge
has rendered them incapable of sinning. John commented that to claim that we have not sinned is
not just to tell a deliberate lie or to be self-deceived,
but to actually accuse God of lying, to "make him
a liar."

Christians sin. The writer encourages "that ye
sin not"; but "if any man sin," there is help. It
is important to keep these two statements in balance. It is possible to be both too severe and too
lenient. Too great a lenience would encourage
Christians to sin. Too great a severity would deny
the possibility of a Christian's sinning.

God's provision for the sinning Christian is in
Jesus—his righteous life, his substitutionary death,
and his heavenly intercession. Each depends on
the other. He could not be our advocate, interced-
ing for us in heaven today, if he had not died for
our sins on Calvary; and his death would have been
useless had his character and life not been perfect.

John continued by saying, "Here are the tests by which we can make sure that we know Him."

The first test is: "We do know that we know him, if we keep his commandments" (1 John 2:3). If we obey him we can claim to know him. This does not mean that only those who keep the commandments perfectly can have assurance, but those who strive, according to human capacity, to conform their lives to the life of Christ. "Whoso keepeth his word" (observing not only his commands but also his word, which reveals his will) shows, by his obedience, that he is a true Christian. True love for God is not expressed in sentimental language but in moral obedience. The proof of love is loyalty. We cannot claim to belong to him unless we behave like him.

The second test is love. "I write no new commandment unto you, but an old commandment which ye had from the beginning. The old commandment is the word which ye have heard from the beginning. Again, a new commandment I write unto you, which thing is true in him and in you: because the darkness is past, and the true light now shineth. He that saith he is in the light, and hateth his brother, is in darkness even until now. He that loveth his brother abideth in the light, and there is none occasion of stumbling in him. But he that hateth his brother is in darkness, and walketh in darkness, and knoweth not whether he goeth, because that darkness hath blinded his eyes" (1 John 2:7-11).

If we love people, we study how to avoid hurting them. Hatred distorts our perspective. "It is love which sees straight, thinks clearly, and makes plans to help."

We are to love God, love each other, and abstain from loving the world. These commandments are keepable because God-given love is not an uncontrollable emotion but a controlled act of the will. If a Christian is engrossed in the pursuits of the world while claiming to serve Christ, it is evident that he has no love for the Father.

John selected three distinct ways to love this world. The first is "the lust of the flesh," which describes the desire of our sinful nature. The second is through "the lust of the eyes." This is the temptation that assaults us from without—through the eyes. Three biblical illustrations of this are: (1) The fruit of the forbidden tree in the garden of Eden was a temptation to Eve through the lust of the eyes; (2) "the goodly Babylonish garment" among the spoil at Jericho was a lust of the eyes to Achan; and (3) Bathsheba as she bathed was a lust of the eyes to David. One writer describes it as "the love of beauty divorced from the love of goodness."

The third way to love the world is through "the pride of life." This is an arrogance related to one's external circumstances, whether wealth or rank or dress. It is the desire to outshine others in luxurious living. Findlay summarizes John's three ways to love the world as "two lusts and one vaunt, two forms of depravation arising from our needs and one from our possessions—unholy desire for things one has not and unholy pride in things one has."

The third test is a doctrinal one. John stated that certain church members had departed from the group. His deduction was, "They were not of us; for if they had been of us, they would no doubt have continued with us" (1 John 2:19). Their departure was their unmasking. Some important light is shed by this verse upon two important doctrines: (1) the perseverance of the saints and (2) the nature of the church. "He that shall endure unto the end, the same shall be saved" (Mark 13:13)—not because salvation is the reward of endurance but because endurance is the hallmark of the saved. Perseverance is the ultimate test of a salvation experience. God intends for his church to be a visible manifestation of an invisible work of grace in the heart. But only the Lord knows "them that are his" (2 Tim. 2:19).

There are some who "share the earthly pilgrimage who do not share the heavenly birth. But those who share the heavenly birth also share the earthly pilgrimage." Only on the final day of separation will the wheat and tares be revealed. Meanwhile, some are "made manifest" by their defection. The false teaching of those who left the church was revealed by John. It is a denial "that Jesus is the Christ." They have taught that Jesus was a mere man who for brief periods of time was given divine powers; but they denied that Jesus and the eternal Son were the same person. They denied the incarnation.

If we claim to enjoy fellowship with God while we walk in sin, "we lie."

If we say we know God but disobey his commandments, "we lie."

If we deny that Jesus is the Christ, we are "the

liar par excellence, the arch-liar, a living embodi-
ment of the spirit of Antichrist."

It isn't enough just to identify these sins and their
circumstances; we must establish safeguards against
them.

First, we must remain true to "That which was
from the beginning" (1 John 1:1).

This is the gospel, the original message that was
preached. We must let it abide in us. It does not
remain automatically. Christians are to be conser-
vative in their theology. They cannot have "itching
ears," forever running after new ideas, which the
apostle Paul said is characteristic of the "perilous
times" of the last days.

Second, the apostolic teaching is not in itself
enough to keep us in the truth. It is possible for
the Christian to be deceived by false teachers. John
said that a second safeguard is "the anointing which
ye have received." Jesus promised that the Holy
Spirit, the Spirit of Truth, would lead "into all of
the Truth."

Here, then, are the two safeguards against the
sin of error—the apostolic Word and the anointing
Spirit. Both are received at conversion. Both are
to be personally grasped and kept in balance. Some
honor the Word and neglect the Spirit who alone
can interpret it; others honor the Spirit but neglect
the Word out of which he teaches.

John emphasized that since Christ is righteous,
we must practice righteousness if we do not want
to be ashamed at his coming. He also encourages
an indispensable necessity for holy living, not on
the expectation of the coming again of the Lord

but from the purpose of his first coming (which was to remove sins through his death).

To continue to live a habitually sinful life is to be completely opposed to the whole purpose of Christ's sacrificial death. It is not just that sin manifests itself in disregard for God's commandment, but that sin in its very nature is lawlessness. Lawlessness is the essence, not the result, of sin. This shows the seriousness of sin. It is more than a personality problem or an innate weakness. Sin is an active rebellion against God. Only when we acknowledge this fact do we take the first step toward holy living.

A sinful life and a Christian life are irreconcilably at enmity with each other. Christians must not compromise with either sin or the devil, or they will find themselves fighting against Christ. If the first step toward holy living is to recognize the sinfulness of sin, the second step is to see its absolute incompatibility with the sinless person and saving work of Jesus.

The believer may fall into sin, but he will not live in it.

Fasting, then, becomes most important as the child of God seeks to uncover and repent of every sin, iniquity, and transgression that lies unnoticed in his life.

5 Different Kinds of Fasts

The Diet Fast

As I continued to examine the facts, it dawned on me that fasting was used by different people to produce different benefits. First, I found several articles recommending the fast to lose weight. Of course, this has nothing to do with the spiritual life, but I wanted to look into it. I knew there was a possible application to the Christian, as obesity has placed many a Christian in a premature grave. The body, "the temple of the Holy Spirit," must be protected. This is the day of diets, but fasting seems to be a rather dramatic way to lose weight.

Across this nation I have talked to scores of people who have tried every possible means of losing weight. They range from those only a few pounds overweight to the obese, some of them 100 pounds or more overweight. Many of these people have come to loathe and despise themselves because of their appearance. Day by day they have less and less self-esteem.

One totally frustrated man said, "I'll go on these fancy crash diets. I'll lose dramatically. But then I'll turn right around and gain all of the weight back—*plus more*!" With deep embarrassment one woman (representative of many to whom I have talked) blurted out her tale of woe: "I've tried it all. I've exercised. Taken drugs. Gone on every fad diet. I've gone to spas. Couldn't even get started losing weight. I just gave up and decided to go to a gland doctor [endocrinologist]. He didn't find anything wrong with my glands!"

As far as weight loss, some people have lost as much as fifteen to seventeen pounds on a five-day fast. Many of them have done it with no bad side-effects and no "withdrawal symptoms" away from food. Some who fast, from time to time, to lose weight report that their eating habits and preferences change and that they are able to keep the weight off due to new tastes and appetites.

Arthur Blessitt, one of my best friends, has (as mentioned before) practiced fasting for years. He related that he has experienced one or two pounds of weight loss per day for several days (I'm sure this depends on the physical condition of the person); then it decreased to about a pound per day.

One of my heroes in the ministry is Charles Haddon Spurgeon. This successful English preacher pastored the Metropolitan Tabernacle in London. The auditorium seated five thousand and was filled to capacity almost every time it was opened. The members of the church were given admission tickets, and the doors were opened to the public only minutes before the service began. His ministry and writings have inspired millions, yet he dug his grave with a knife and fork, dying of obesity at the age of fifty-eight.

Obviously, too much food can hurt the body.

What about too little? I began to gather information from the medical profession.

One medical journal reports that patients who fast undergo quite a change in eating habits, and that the patients' main benefit has been better feelings and a better self-image.

People who gain weight, sometimes seemingly without large amounts of food, most likely have sluggish metabolism. The glucose in their systems is changed to fat too quickly, so an imbalance results. Fasting can sometimes make changes which help the person with a low metabolic rate.

It is a common medical fact that changes brought about by fasting can help weight loss even after a person is off the fast.

There are dangers to the diet fast. Most apparent, of course, is the danger that a person will find out he can lose in a hurry—without hunger pains. Such a person could do considerable harm to his health without the supervision of a physician.

Even though I have not fasted for dieting purposes, I have been happy with my weight loss during my fasts. Because of my travels—eating out, banquets, brunches, the circuit—I look upon losing a few pounds as an added dividend to the spiritual blessings which I derive from the practice.

Many doctors have reported that patients who fast feel a euphoria, a sense of victory and mastery over themselves. They say to themselves, ''I never thought that I could do without food for more than one or two meals. Now I am able to stick with it—and enjoy it—for three, maybe four days."

Another benefit of fasting is teaching oneself. Fasting can do what regular diets or "programs" cannot, or seldom, do—it helps "foodaholics" to adopt discipline about a low-calorie diet.

Many people ask, "If I lose weight by fasting, will I regain it in a hurry?" Of course, since I have never fasted for the purpose of losing weight, I can't answer first-hand. Studies at several universities, however, have shown that a large number of people who lose weight by fasting kept their weight down or continued to lose.

It is estimated by insurance companies that 65 to 70 percent of the population is overweight. We are told by many medical authorities that these people are in serious condition. First, they are constantly tired, because they are carrying around too many pounds. Let us say that a person is forty pounds overweight. If a normal person carried around a forty-pound sack of potatoes all day, he would be exhausted. This is a poor analogy, but it illustrates the problem. Then again for every cubic inch of fat on the overweight person, the body must have 700 miles (not a misprint) of fine tubes to nourish and sustain this excess fat. There is a tremendous burden placed on the lungs and heart.

Something needs to be done about overweight.

The Ritual Fast

The educational center of the world was at one time Alexandria, Egypt. Before students were permitted to study with the masters of the world, they were forced to fast for forty days.

Buddha and Gandhi fasted for long periods of time. The influential religious leaders had great confidence in the power of fasting—not to improve the physical body but to have a keener understanding of the Person higher than ourselves—to create a higher mental power.

Religious people of the East have practiced fasting as a ritual for a long time. They practiced fasting not only for the recovery of health but for spiritual illumination as well. Pythagoras required his disciples to undertake a forty-day fast before they could be initiated into the mysteries of his occult philosophical teachings. He claimed that only through this experience could their minds be sufficiently purified and clarified to receive and understand the profound teaching of the mysteries of life.

Other Fasts

Tremendous distress, such as the death of a loved one or another trauma, can cause the loss of appetite and lead to a form of fasting. Hannah was disturbed because of her childlessness and "wept, and did not eat" (1 Sam. 1:7). David showed his grief by fasting following Abner's death. (2 Sam. 3:35).

In Ezra 10:6 and Esther 4:3 it is not certain whether fasting is used religiously or as an expression of sorrow. The mourning customs of ancient days nearly always included fasting.

Fasting was used as a religious act and as a funeral custom. Second Samuel 12:16–23 records the unusual behavior of David. David fasted and mourned while his child was extremely ill. When the child died, though, he dressed up, dried his tears, and ordered a sumptious feast. His servants could not understand. He defended his fasting *before* and not after the child's death on the grounds that, while the child was alive, his prayer might be answered. His fasting was intended to help his prayers.

At times fasting was proclaimed on a national scale (Jud. 20:26, 2 Chron. 20:3, Joel 1:13).

Fasting could be partial—for instance, abstinence from certain kinds of food—or total—for instance, abstinence from all food, as well as from sleeping and bathing, etc.

The Hebrews saw a close connection between fasting and spiritual and intellectual awareness.

6 Messages From People Who Fast

Fasting can be found in nearly all religions, philosophies, and moral codes. Zoroaster, the influential Persian prophet, taught and practiced fasting. So did Socrates, Aristotle, and Plato. The father of medicine, Hippocrates, considered fasting to be the great natural healer. Leonardo da Vinci practiced and advocated fasting. Confucius fasted and encouraged it. The Yogis of India practice fasting as a means of spiritual enlightenment. The greatest modern example of a fast-er is Mahatma Gandhi.

The founders of Judaism, Christianity, Buddhism, and Islam taught fasting as a means of communication with the divine through purification of body, mind, and spirit . . . to be carried out with dedication and in private.

Many outstanding Christian leaders have made fasting a part of their discipline. It is impossible for me to place a complete list of them in this book, but I will mention a few of them: Arthur Blessitt, Corrie ten Boom, Ron Lewis, Billy Graham, Paul Ragland, Percy Ray, Lester Roloff, Aubert Rose, Charles Stanley, James Smith, and Jack Taylor.

In the following pages you will find some personal testimonies from a few of these personalities.

I am also including some excerpts from my personal diary. Space would not permit me to recall all of the experiences I have had as a fast-er, but the following are selected from my diary. They express some of my learning-developing experiences. These are undated for obvious reasons.

At this point in my fasting experience I know very little. I know I can refrain from eating solid foods for a period of time without injuring my body, but I cannot live without water. God would not ask me to do something that would injure the "temple of the Holy Spirit"—my body.

Arthur Blessitt walked into my life several weeks ago. He practices fasting. As I study his life, I find that he is one of the most genuine Christians I've met. I wonder if fasting has helped produce this spirit? I will know later as I plan to interview him.

The Holy Spirit has begun to zero in on me again about fasting. My prayer life has been a rich experience for many years as I try to spend one to two hours a day with the Lord. How precious this time has become. Most of my "devotional dews" and sermons have come from these extended times with Jesus. When I fail to have this time of prayer and study, I feel like chaff. There is no germinating power to help me grow or enrich the lives of others. The Spirit will not leave me alone. I will act—I will fast.

This fast is not an experiment but an experience.

I do not fast to test God but to know God. I will fast until God has obtained his goal for this experience. This is not an endurance test to see *if* I can fast until God says, "Stop." I fast to know the will of God for me. This is not a time of crisis or great decision, but a time of total commitment of myself to God. He is my Lord. I am ready to follow my leader wherever he leads. For some reason—unknown to me—God has placed me in a position of leadership. I cannot lead without a leader. I must keep my eyes on the author-finisher of my faith.

For the last few days I have been impressed to fast. This thirst is ever present. Before going to bed last night I told my wife not to prepare breakfast for me as I was beginning a fast. I was overwhelmed to fast and pray for three things as the New Year approached:

1. "That I may know him, the power of his resurrection and the fellowship of his suffering."

2. For my people, Southern Baptists, for a spiritual awakening.

3. For America, for a genuine revival of Bible study.

It is my intention to read the Gospels during this fast. This will help me to know Jesus better.

This has been an unusual day. During the breakfast hour I read Matthew 2. In verses 12-15 the blessed Lord showed me some truths about the detours of life. The detour is ordained of God vv. 12-13); the time is selected by God (vv. 12-13); the destination is chosen by God (v. 13); the purpose is known by God (v. 13); and the end is determined by God (v. 15). Thank you, Lord, for this time of fasting and quietness.

I have been burdened to fast and pray for two things.

1. That God will fulfill a financial need during September.

"Seek ye first the kingdom of God and all these things will be added unto you." I seek the kingdom of God and am depending on him to supply the need.

2. On Friday night I will speak to the leadership of more than one hundred churches. This will kick off a large ACTION program.

In past experience with simultaneous associational programs, we have experienced a growth of approximately one hundred per church. Since there are over one million unreached people in the area covered by these churches, I am burdened that God will give even a larger number of enrollees. Oh, it will take a large hell just to hold the lost of this one area if we fail. My fasting is such a small price to pay for so many.

Throughout the afternoon I wrestled with God in prayer. At times there was no sign of victory, but just before sundown the Son came down and bathed me with his presence. Much time passed, but it seemed like only a moment. The hyssop was dipped in the blood of Jesus and applied to my life. I was clean. Access into the holy of holies became real. A complete assurance swept over me that the September financial needs were already taken care of. As I write this account I have no idea how it will be done, but I know it will. The burden is gone. (God supplied every need during the first week in September.)

It will be over two weeks before I will receive the final results of the simultaneous ACTION meetings; but that, too, will be accomplished. Oh! the blessedness of God's assurance. (Everyone involved in these meetings was astonished at the increase. To God be the glory.)

My family came to mind during this sweet hour of prayer. God is caring for them while I travel. I also prayed for two new friends—a pastor and a lawyer—who are critically ill. I wrestled with God for their health. By nightfall it was over. The victories had become realities, and I slept in peace.

Upon arriving at Glorieta (Southern Baptist conference center) on Friday, I was awed by the presence of the Holy Spirit ministering to me. It was not from the fact that this is such an inspiring place, but there has been an urgency here which I rarely experience. I ate my evening meal with Alvis Strickland, adult consultant at the Sunday School Board. I knew this would be my last meal for a while as I had to fast.

Most of my time during the last four days has been spent in Bible study, prayer, and meditation, although I have also carried a heavy schedule of conference leading. I sought God. I wanted to see his smile. I dug the sins out of my life. I found many petty things, all of which were evil in God's sight. One by one I confessed them.

Several people have remarked that I looked tired. A better word would have been *burdened*. They didn't realize what was taking place.

It is now the following Wednesday. The fast has continued through these days. Last night I had a definite assurance of God's presence. After the evening worship service I returned to my room, not taking time to fellowship with others. As I prayed for relief from the heavy burden, it came. I could almost hear God say, "Son, it is enough. I have heard and answered."

My life and attitude have been totally changed by the fasting experiences of the last four years. I state some of these benefits in a following chapter.

Jack R. Taylor

I believe fasting to be feasible. This is neither a condemnation on those who do not practice it nor a commendation of those who do. It is a personal assessment and a personal report. I have dealt with this subject in the book *Much More.*

I practice fasting on occasions, always with great profit and blessing. I plan to do it more because lately it seems to be more on my heart. I have engaged in several types of fasting. I have, over periods of time, fasted regularly one day a week.

At other times I have gone for a two- or three-day period for special reasons—some important decision, consideration, or problem. There have been a few times when I have engaged in what I call "preoccupation" fasting. God was dealing with me in such a way that I did not think of food and thus needed none.

The fact that I included the subject of fasting in the book *Much More* would indicate that fasting would likely be a dimension of growth in the spiritual life. If I were you, I would not force the subject if I had never fasted, but I would ask the Lord what he wanted to teach me on the subject. I believe that blessings will be forthcoming.

Physically, mentally, and spiritually, fasting has an immediate reward. I believe that a new assessment needs to be made on the part of the Christian in the use of the body to God's glory. Aside from the spiritual benefits of fasting, many years may be added to a believer's life by periodic fasting and proper eating habits.

I commend fasting to you as a means of deeper concentration on the things of the Lord, as a means of liberation from the tyranny of the taste buds, and as a means of physical renewal.

Jack R. Taylor is the president of Dimensions in Christian Living, San Antonio, Texas.

Arthur Blessitt

In the Bible we find several occasions where

fasting preceded significant events. As an illustration, Moses fasted and prayed for forty days before the Ten Commandments were given. Also, Jesus fasted and prayed for forty days before he began his public ministry. It seems to have been this same pattern of fasting and prayer that has marked several significant experiences in my life.

In 1969 I fasted and prayed on the Sunset Strip for twenty-eight days. We had been evicted from our building by the surrounding nightclubs because they considered our witnessing for Christ a public nuisance. The entire witness of Jesus on the sin-filled Sunset Strip was at stake. We took the twelve-foot cross from our building, and, chained to the front of the cross, I fasted and prayed that the witness of Jesus would not be driven from the streets of Hollywood and that we might have a building made available to us. We wanted to continue "His Place," our Jesus nightclub on the Sunset Strip.

I was on the street in this public place twenty-four hours a day. As I prayed, God's Spirit drew thousands of people who wanted to talk. We saw hundreds saved, including the well-known writer Bob Friedman, who was a news reporter for the *Los Angeles Herald-Examiner*. My own life was enriched beyond measure. I was praying and fasting for a specific purpose. On the evening of the twenty-seventh day, a man came up to me and said, "I'll rent you a new building tomorrow." The witness of Jesus has continued on the Sunset Strip, where now only one out every four nightclubs which were open in 1969 remain open.

In July, 1970, I arrived in Washington, D.C. after walking across America with the same twelve-foot cross. My wife and I fasted and prayed for forty days in Washington, D.C. at the corner of Fifteenth and Constitution Avenues. Day and night we prayed and shared Christ with people. We saw hundreds of people come to Christ; yet our main burden in this fast was that God would cleanse the White House and then put into office an open follower of Jesus Christ and send a revival and awakening to this nation.

It's been a number of years since we fasted forty days in Washington. God has exposed the sin in the White House. There has been a cleansing in Washington; and a president who openly declares that he is born again is now in the high office of our nation.

In the fast that the Lord leads me to take, we only drink water or sometimes a cold drink. I never eat any food or take vitamins or any juice or nourishment. The body is made for a perfect forty-day fast. At the conclusion of these long fasts, I ate fried chicken to end one fast and roast beef to end the other. Both of these fasts have been outdoors for me; I slept in a sleeping bag on the streets in a public place.

There have been only a few occasions besides the Washington trip when God has led me to fast. Since space is limited, I shall only mention one other. That occurred when I set up the cross in the middle of the battlefield in North Ireland and fasted and prayed for three days. The fighting at the moment has not yet ended in that troubled land, but one of greatest stirs of spiritual revival that I know of anywhere is taking place there.

In my personal life, fasting has been for specific purposes and for a long duration. After three days, there are no hunger pains or desire for food. From twelve to fourteen days later, there seems to be a sense of complete cleanliness and mental clarity. After twenty-one days, there seems to be an outpouring of spiritual power and creativity that is indescribable, but that continues until the fast is ended. It seems especially after the third week that one is no longer even remotely interested in the trivial physical world around. One's mind is filled exclusively with profound spiritual ideas and truths.

One of the most profound things is that the mind will concentrate for hours on the same subject without once wavering or being distracted. There is no question that there is awesome power in fasting. If the fast is controlled by the Holy Spirit and Jesus is foremost, then it is a beautiful and powerful experience. However, if it is not, be warned because non-Spirit-controlled fasting can open the mind and body to the control of evil spirits. Note the conditions and places surrounding Mohammed, Gandhi, various gurus, and others. Long fasts are inherently spiritual; but if you take one, make sure that you are completely committed to Jesus. Otherwise, it is the most dangerous thing you could attempt.

Arthur Blessitt is an evangelist from Hollywood, California.

Aubert Rose

I became interested in fasting about seven years ago while I was a pastor in Ohio. Dr. Charles Stanley came and preached three sermons to our pastor's conference, and all three were on fasting. At that time the Lord put it on my heart to become a fast-er. Dr. Stanley reminded us that there were some things we could never know about God if we were not willing to be obedient in this aspect of our lives. Since I've had a hunger to know all there is to know about God, I could hardly wait to get started.

I began fasting. I had a hard time even sharing it with my wife for fear of bragging about what I was doing. My wife does not worry a lot about my eating; but on that day she, not knowing what I was doing, tried to feed me all day. I finally had to tell her I was fasting. She joined me.

For a long time I fasted one day each week, on my day off—the day I worked harder, physically. I drank a lot of water and fasted food. I became totally convinced that doing so was good for my health. It definitely helped the digestion of my food. It made my food taste better. I was surprised to discover how much time I spent in eating. On the day I fasted, I spent this time in Bible reading, meditation, prayer, and searching for the Lord's will in my life.

At our church we fast on special occasions. Sometimes we challenge the members to fast for one day. Our staff has fasted one day a month, the first Friday, for a long time.

Some of the physical effects I've noticed are a slight headache and a slight desire for food, but no dizziness or weakness and no waning of energy.

One of the spiritual benefits is that I have learned who is in control of my life. Christ, not appetite, tells me what to do. Fasting is a step of obedience; and when we obey God, there is a great sense of satisfaction. Another spiritual benefit is increased discipline.

I heartily recommend fasting to everyone unless there is a physical problem involved. It is a step toward obedience and discipline, which all Christians need to develop more fully.

Aubert Rose is the assistant pastor, First Baptist Church, Atlanta, Georgia.

Dr. Charles Stanley

Fasting is not a matter of law. It was practiced by both Old Testament personalities and New Testament personalities. It is practiced by people today. And it has a tremendous effect on the life of the person who practices it.

Fasting is never done alone; it is always accompanied by prayer.

When someone says, "I don't think it is important to fast today," I urge him to examine the Scriptures to discover that the men of God who made an imprint for God were men who fasted.

The purpose of fasting is not to persuade God to do something against his will. Once in a while someone says, "I have prayed and prayed, and nothing has happened. I'm going to fast. If I fast, God is obligated to do what I want. No, he isn't. God's will should be of primary importance in our lives. The result of fasting is what happens to us, not to him.

There are several reasons for fasting:

1. The ultimate reason should be that we are so burdened about something, so concerned about it, that we lose our appetites. Replacing the physical appetite should be a deep, insatiable, moaning, groaning hunger for God.

2. There should be a desire to make ourselves available to God. Fasting is not done for the purpose of doing something for God; it is done for the purpose of doing something for ourselves. The end result is that we are more available to God. He can work through us.

3. There should be a desire to improve our physical health. Some people fast in order to lose weight. And if you have a problem with that, let me tell you a healthy thing. I believe that if you fast one day a week, in a period of a few weeks or months, God will honor your sincerity. If your motive is to get yourself in the kind of physical condition to be more available to God, you will lose weight. Of course, you don't want to fast if you have some physical problems that would be aggravated by fasting or if you are under a doctor's order to eat at a regular schedule.

4. A primary reason to fast is to discipline the human body. You can discover who is in control of your life when you decide to fast for several

days. About 5 o'clock on the first afternoon you will tell yourself you are about to collapse for lack of food. Here is why. You say to yourself, *I've got terrible hunger pains; I've just got to eat.* For the first twenty-four hours you don't have a hunger pain because you are not hungry. Look at yourself. You've got enough fat to last you a pretty good while without getting hungry. What you really feel is the time clock in your body. Haven't you heard people say, "My, it's 6 o'clock and time to eat"? All of a sudden you are gripped with an uncontrollable hunger. It has nothing to do with your stomach; it is in the head. We are controlled by our appetites more than we want to admit.

Throughout the Bible we find God's men disciplining their bodies and bringing their desires under control by fasting. Fasting will bring the human body under divine control. God desires that nothing but the Holy Spirit control us. If man's body is not under control, neither is his spirit. The Holy Spirit controls the whole person or he controls none of the person. If you do not bring the total body under control, you will lose control of what you do have control of. No one can be disciplined in one part of his life and undisciplined in another part. There is no such thing as a partially disciplined person. One of the most important things about fasting is that it shapes us and gets us under God's control.

5. Another reason to fast is that it helps us discover the will of God. Here is the place God has taught me the most. If you don't ever fast for any other reason, teenagers, begin fasting now to get

the mind of God for your life. You are not fasting to get God to show you something he doesn't want to show you. You are setting aside time to concentrate on God and remain in his presence long enough for him to instruct you. If you will fast to find the mind of God, I guarantee that it will come crystal clear. You will face the world and never fudge an inch because you will know you got your information from God.

6. We should fast during repentance. This does not mean we cannot be forgiven unless we fast, but there are times when it seems we cannot accept God's forgiveness. Fasting doesn't force God to forgive you; fasting sets your mind toward God. When you think as he thinks, you think forgiveness.

7. We should fast when we are concerned for God's work. I believe the greatest thing a church could have is a staff, deacons, and leaders who fast and pray—not when the church burns down, but in order to get the church on fire. A lot of dead churches would catch fire if the people in places of leadership would set aside a period of time for fasting and prayer.

8. We should fast for protection. In 2 Chronicles 20 we find that Jehoshaphat did this. "Then there came some that told Jehoshaphat, saying, There cometh a great multitude against thee from beyond the sea on this side Syria; and, behold, they be in Hazazon-tamar . . . . And Jehoshaphat feared, and set himself to seek the Lord, and proclaimed a fast throughout all Judah" (vv. 2-3).

9. Fasting brings about a supernatural work in our lives. God will not entrust supernatural power

to those whose lives are not under total control. Why would God want to release his supernatural energy, supernatural power, supernatural demonstration of himself to a person who could not even control his own appetite? What would happen? That person would begin to use God. And God isn't going to be used by anyone. The Christian who would have the supernatural power of God must be under the total control of the Holy Spirit.

10. We should fast to understand the Scriptures. How often, when we cannot understand a certain Bible verse, do we run to a commentary? If we would fast and pray we would see, feel, hear, and touch things on the pages of God's Word we would never experience at any other time. There is something awesome about getting everything else out of the way and concentrating on God.

Fast privately—let it be between you and God. Then, in God's time, He will publicly reward you. He will do something to your countenance, your energy, your witness, your influence, your life that will be very demonstrative.

Dr. Charles Stanley is the pastor, First Baptist Church, Atlanta, Georgia.

Dr. James Smith

The subject of fasting has never been a matter of deep personal conviction with me. In my background I have somewhat glossed over the passages relating to fasting. In the case of David in his fasting and mourning prior to the death of his son, I realize that here was a man emotionally overcome—not only with personal grief but also with the realization that what was happening to the child was the direct result of his own sin. Therefore, he basically had no desire for food. This, very frankly, has been my background interpretation of the passages of Scripture related to fasting. My answer has always been that if a person becomes so burdened, feels so distressed, or has such a sense of guilt about his relationship to God that he has lost his appetite for food, he should give priority to reconciling his life to God or to solving what has the priority in his life.

The passage of Scripture that has been most difficult for me to get around is the statement made by Jesus in the Sermon on the Mount—Matthew 6:16-18. Jesus began by saying, "When you fast." Not *if* you fast, but *when.* The implication is that there comes a time in every serious, sincere believer's life when he fasts; and I realize that this is a direct and specific teaching of our Lord. Therefore, this verse caused me to pursue the subject deeper than I had done in former times. I am convinced that fasting should be considered one of the disciplines of the Christian life. In the passage in Matthew 6, it is related to the disciplines of praying and giving. Therefore, there should be some degree of frequency about the practice.

In the more recent years of my life and ministry, I have come to realize the strong adversary that we have in the flesh. According to Galatians 5:16, the flesh has a strong desire to suppress the Spirit, and the Spirit has a strong desire to suppress the flesh. These opponents are in a state of open warfare. Every Christian must face this conflict and realize that there are places where we must take a stand to actually say no to the flesh. This perhaps more than any other one thing caused me to take the initial step of setting aside a time every week in which I actually fast for at least two meals, and usually three. This time is usually from noon Sunday until dinner on Monday evening.

For years I have had low blood pressure, and the result is a sense of tiredness most of the time. My doctors have often said that no one ever dies from low blood pressure, but that I'll be tired the rest of my life. They have also encouraged me, when I begin to feel unusually tired, to drink a cup of coffee or eat something. It seems that my ability to derive energy from my food is almost instantaneous. Therefore, I had become convinced that if I did without a meal I would probably get so weak that I couldn't live. The truth of the matter is that it has been the other way around. I have been literally amazed that once I had set myself to the practice, I found that I have not been hungry. Nor have I felt a sense of weakness; nor do I feel that it has been in any way a detriment to my physical health and well-being. If anything, it has probably had the opposite effect. On these days there is a real sense of victory—especially over the flesh.

It is good to exercise a discipline in which you are really denying self in saying no to the flesh and at the same time saying yes to the Lord. You are putting a priority on the Spirit instead of on the flesh.

Dr. James Smith is the executive secretary of the Illinois Baptist State Association.

Ron Lewis

Early Concepts of Fasting

Born and raised as a Southern Baptist, I have had rather negative attitudes concerning fasting. I had never properly understood the concept of fasting or the theology that is involved. I still don't; but what ideas I have had concerning fasting were negative until about a year and a half ago.

In reality I considered fasting outside my theological perspective, mainly because I have never studied its place in the Christian experience. I had stumbled across it in trying to preach a sermon that dealt with Mark 9:17-29. In this passage a boy was healed, and Jesus told the disciples that one of the reasons they could not perform the miracle of healing was because that kind of healing came only by prayer and fasting. In delivering that sermon I usually avoided addressing myself to the portion of the text that included the term fasting.

Another reason fasting was outside my theological perspective was that I never considered myself to be a very pious or holy Christian. I have always had a different kind of stance than people who pursued deeper life experiences with Christ. I do consider myself to have a very deep personal relationship with Jesus Christ as he is revealed in the Word of God. I do accept him as God in the flesh, and I have accepted him as my Savior and my Lord. It seemed to me that the models of people who were involved in deep spiritual experiences were of such a different nature than mine that I considered fasting more for persons with that type of spiritual experience rather than for someone like me.

Out of the background of these early concepts grew what I call my basic introduction to fasting.

Basic Introduction to Fasting

Even though I have entered into the fasting experience, I still have not built a strong theology that I would recommend to other people. The fasting experience, I think, is a deeply personal matter. It is probably best dealt with by explanations that are less formal than the preaching situation. A person needs time to explain fully his motives and experiences. This seems necessary so people will not assume that one is searching for some type of second or third level of blessing from God.

Basic introductions to fasting come through discussions with other people. Most of them I found while discussing fasting with people who were approaching it from the same or a similar perspective. That means that it was more or less a teaching that was not necessarily primary in the Bible and therefore was designed only for a select few to experience. I treated it more or less like the experience in John 13, which deals with the washing of feet.

In a casual conversation with a personal friend, driving from an airport in St. Louis, I had noted in a message he had delivered that he had referred to the experience of fasting. He had not made a major issue of it. So I picked up on it to see if he would elaborate. My friend was very gracious about it and approached fasting from a very commonsense point of view. He did not elaborate on the super spiritual side of fasting; he spoke of it only as a very rich, rewarding, and personal experience. He did not have a sensational spiritual experience to attach to it. He only made it clear that it had been a blessing along with many other blessings in his spiritual life.

What Precipitated the Fasting?

In the fall of 1975 I began a very deep and personal struggle for an identity insofar as my relationship with Christ, my calling, and vocation were concerned. My experience began growing from the casual conversation I had had with this friend. It had been fermenting for about a year. The time came when I was elk hunting on the side of a mountain in Southern Colorado one October. The snow was about waist deep, and I found a rock jutting out from under the snow. I sat down on that rock to talk to God and to praise him for the beauty and splendor before me. In my heart there was a deep longing to know who I was and what God had planned for me.

The first day on the continental divide I sat on that rock and said, "God, this week I am going to reduce all my requests into one. And the request is that you might not let me die until I know why I lived in the first place." That prayer I prayed time and time again during the week.

I left the mountains without my answer. I would have to admit that I was deeply disappointed. I did not have the peace I was looking for; nor did I have the clear-cut answer I felt I deserved.

Driving back to Illinois, I had a lot of time to think about why God did not answer the prayers as I thought he should. I began to discover some truths about myself. One of the things I discovered was that I have a tendency to tell God how to run his business.

In a search for the ultimate meaning of life I went from October until February struggling, grasping, looking, reading, searching, and praying. The cycle repeated itself over and over again. I was bitterly disappointed in the type of feedback I was getting from my reading, discussions with people, and prayer time with God.

During the last weekend of January I encountered my friend again. I slipped over to one side of the room and told him that he and I needed to talk privately after the sessions were over. He and I sought out a motel room where we could discuss privately this experience of fasting.

Needless to say, my ignorance of the subject was and still is profound, but I found myself filled with many questions. I had experienced going hungry many times in my life and dreaded the piercing headaches, the pains in the stomach, and the weakening sensations during the day. I dreaded the grouchiness that usually went with my getting hungry and the growling of my stomach. I asked questions concerning my health, how fasting would affect my attitude, and how I would explain to people when I did not eat—the same questions people have been asking about fasting for a long time. My friend answered with common sense and in a very Christian and understanding way. He was kind and patient with me and assured me that there was no danger to my health as long as I was careful to keep my body filled with liquids. He also assured me not to worry about what people thought because there were always ways to explain why you were not eating without trying to present yourself as being a super spiritual person.

I started my fast that very day. It was Saturday.

The Experience of Fasting

The first day was not very difficult except for the times when we were around other people. I would order something cool or warm to drink. The second day I got up in the morning, wondering if I could survive without breakfast. It was astonishing. All I had was a glass of orange juice and a cup of tea. I was well on my way to a fast. The day passed on; the noon hour came; and again I took some liquid refreshment. The same thing occurred in the evening.

I probably should insert here what I was trying to accomplish during the fast. I was seeking God's purpose and plan for my life. My plan was to use fasting as a means of focusing my mind entirely on that very issue. My friend had assured me if I could experience fasting, I would probably experience a focusing of my attention on certain areas of my life in such a way as I had never dreamed possible. He was right.

But I had a second reason for the fast. I was presenting a paper to the editors and consultants of the Baptist Sunday School Board. This paper contained the conviction of a basic need for cross-cultural curriculum for Southern Baptists if we were going to address the gospel to the millions of cross-cultural people in America in the next twenty-five years. Accompanied with that was the fact that I had an appointment with Dr. Grady C. Cothen and Dr. William O. Thomason to discuss the issues of church growth as they relate to Southern Baptists in America and around the world. So in reality my fast had a twofold purpose. Both of them were extremely important to my life and pilgrimage.

I anticipated that the answers would be very clear and concise. I would walk out of the experience with every assurance that my life was perfectly planned and that I would know what that plan was. A secondary benefit would be a pleasant reception by the editors and consultants and at least a hearing by Dr. Cothen and Dr. Thomason.

The real issue at stake was the discovery of my identity and God's plan for my life.

I arrived home and tried to explain to my wife what I was trying to accomplish. In her wisdom she said, "I hope you won't expect too much." Those are words that every person who tries fasting should take with great seriousness. Do not expect too much from a fast. There are only certain things God wants to do in your life, regardless of whether you are fasting.

The dread of pain from hunger was unfounded. From Saturday until Monday I hardly noticed that I had not eaten.

On Monday I began to experience some of the sensations my friend had indicated. I began to have a change of taste in my mouth. I began to have some physical changes that affected my stomach. I found myself able to concentrate in an unusual way. I was surprised.

It was not easy for me to avoid letting people know I was fasting. There were several parties and get-togethers during that particular week. Finally, in order to clarify things with my own staff, I called together the five men who served with me at that time and explained to them what I was trying to do. Each of them was very affirmative, gracious, and kind.

On Tuesday it was time for me to make my trip to Nashville. I had made arrangements with a close friend at the Baptist Sunday School Board to pick me up at the airport. He was there waiting when I got off the plane. He and I have always enjoyed some of the fine restaurants in Nashville. Too, he is an excellent cook and had always made sure that we had at least one elegant meal in his home if I were to stay in Nashville for any length of time. So I was wondering how I would explain to him my pursuing the experience of fasting. I decided when I got off the plane that I should tell him early in the evening. We got in his car and started backing out from the parking stall. When I told him, his answer was, "I'm fasting, too."

God has never ceased to amaze me at the way he works through his providence to assist his children. Again and again he has stood by me, helped me, and ministered to me. In his gentle, quiet way he affirmed through my friend that I had made the right step in searching for his will through the process of fasting. I was to be the house guest of this friend for the entire week. It made things so much easier.

On Wednesday I took liquid refreshment again and found myself able to conserve an hour and half of every day. We do not realize how much time we spend in thinking about our next meal, going to our next meal, participating in the meal, physically recovering from eating, and digesting. I am confident that fasting added an hour and half to two hours to my productivity each day. The intensity with which I could focus my mind was one of the exciting features of the fasting process. The Word of God became very real and precious during that time. I could read it with clarity because my mind was fixed completely on it.

It was amazing how well I could sleep at night. I anticipated I would dream about food and would crave something to eat. I had none of those sensations. It was a very peaceful time for me. Patience was a by-product of my fasting experience. A sensitivity that I cannot explain was a reality in day-by-day living. The peace with which I approached family challenges and my day-by-day difficulties was very rewarding to me.

I broke the fast on Thursday evening and ate a very light meal. Actually, I felt that it was time.

I did not have a big revelation that it was time for me to quit. I really did not have a sign from someone; nor did I have any pressure put on me by anyone. There was just a peace that came over me, and I took it as an indication that the fasting experience was over for that time.

On Friday I returned home to explain to my wife some of the experiences of the week. I had been well received by the editors of the Sunday School Board and had enjoyed a kind and gracious hearing with Dr. Cothen and Dr. Thomason. The placing of the burden of church growth before these people was one of the real rewarding experiences of my life. But I still did not have clear-cut answers from God concerning life's meanings and the plan God had for my life. I must admit that I was extremely disappointed. I almost felt I had earned the right for God to bless me with clear-cut instructions about my future.

I went through the entire weekend with no clear-cut answers from God. I experienced self-pity and disappointment. On Monday morning while my children were preparing for school, my wife and I were carrying on our usual chitchat conversation. I began to relive my experience. My children listened calmly and had very little to say. I received the customary hug around the neck, a kiss on the cheek, and the assurances they would see me later. Off to school they went. My wife sat down with a cup of coffee, and I opened a translation of the New International Version of the New Testament.

I had before me Hebrews 11 and was glancing through the account of the heroes of faith, with which most of us are at least nominally acquainted. It had little impact on me until I came to the closing verses of the eleventh chapter. Hebrews 11:39 to 12:1 reads as follows: "These were all commended for their faith, yet none of them received what had been promised. God had planned something better for us so that only together with us would they be made perfect. Therefore, since we are surrounded by such a great cloud of witnesses, let us throw off everything that hinders and the sin that so easily entangles us, and let us run with perseverance the race marked out before us."

Verse 40 was the one that stood out to me so much. It contains the fact that we are so intricately related in God's family that not one of us can have the entire purpose and plan of his life placed before him unless all of us have the same privilege. We belong to each other in such sophisticated, complicated, and spiritual ways that no one of us can have all of that revelation because of the effect that it has on all the rest. This word began to reveal to me how closely knit the family of God is. We are blood brothers in Christ. This mystical union is more real than our physical union. God cannot reveal his entire purpose and plan in my life clearly and concisely with no venture of faith on my part because there are too many people with whom I am related.

Epilogue

In all honesty, I cannot recommend fasting for everyone. I do not know the health factors that might be involved for someone else. I do not know the spiritual journeys that others may be traveling. Each one of us is on the spiritual pilgrimage with Christ in different ways. It is regrettable that someone might use it to persuade God that he is committed to him in some special way. It should not be used as a fetish or a spiritual ritual. It should not be an experience that is flaunted in front of other people to prove more spiritual maturity than those who have not experienced it.

Fasting is deeply personal. It is necessary for certain kinds of people who are searching for God in some special way. It is a rich and rewarding experience that brings a kind of peace to your life you never knew existed. It offers a confidence that you can be the master of your appetites if you set your mind and heart on God. Fasting enriches the prayer life and Bible study. It opens doors to spiritual realities about yourself and your relationship with God that might not be opened any other way.

So I do not commend fasting to everyone. But for someone who was, like I, walking in the Christian pilgrimage somewhere in the same level as I, let me commend to you the experience of fasting, in the name of Jesus Christ.

Ron Lewis is the director of the church development division of the Illinois Baptist State Association.

7 Benefits of Fasting

I Am Spiritually Cleaner

No, I have not arrived. I have only begun in the journey toward holiness. The Bible says, "If I regard iniquity in my heart, the Lord will not hear me" (Ps. 66:18). Man's sinful nature has a tendency to hid his sins. It is much easier to confess and forsake sin as soon as it is committed, but man is "prone to backsliding." At least temporarily he feels he can hide it. If it is left unconfessed, it produces a short-circuit between him and God. When it is confessed, it is forgiven. This is where fasting fits in. We are so busy doing church and other good work that we have little time to meditate on our sins and God's holiness. A time of fasting is a time of examination, of scrutiny, when a definite effort is put forth to find, name, and confess every sin—even the little ones.

During my fasts, I ask God to turn on his spiritual spotlight and call to my attention my sins, iniquities, and transgressions. I want to be reminded of the omissions and the commissions. I want to be reminded of every evil thought and act, of wrong motives and attitudes, of "stretched" stories, of lack of Bible study, prayer, personal witness, love, and ego trips. I ask the holy God to let me see myself as he sees me. And you know what? He does! Some of the sins I found in my life were disobeying his specific commands, striving for things on the earth instead of setting my mind on things above, refusing to trust God for the little things as well as the big ones, love for the world—money, fame, popularity, recognition, idolatry, and misusing time, talent, and possessions.

I also found I was not loving others as I should. There were unkind words and acts, a critical spirit, grudges, lack of forgiveness, spite, prejudice, indifference, anxiety, jealousy, irritability, impatience, lust, pride, stinginess, and complacency also harbored in my heart. This was only the beginning of my find.

During the times of fasting and prayer these were confessed—one at a time—and removed by God's forgiving spirit. The result of this experience makes one spiritually cleaner.

I Have Learned a New Discipline

No longer is my life centered around eat and drink. Before the experiences of the last few years, I was a food addict. I ate whether I was hungry or not. It was difficult to go to bed without a snack. Now life is more than just satisfying the physical cravings.

Discipline is hard to achieve for most people, and discipline in relationship to appetite is one of the most difficult to achieve. Ask any obese person.

When I reached middle age I had difficulty with "the middle-age spread." My intake was about the same as when I was younger; but my activity slowed down, which resulted in overweight. Diets were impossible. The basic problem lay in the fact that I was undisciplined. I could not bring my body under subjection. It was an innate weakness combined with a bad habit.

If my only motive were to lose weight, I don't think I could discipline myself to fast. However, when the motive is to obey the will of God and discover a new, fresh cleansing, there is no contest. God supplies the willpower. Once this lesson is learned, the new discipline becomes a reality.

Nowhere in this book have I stated that fasting is easy. I have said it is worth the disciplined effort. Once the appetite is under control, the rest of the undisciplined areas of life can be controlled.

I Have Discovered a More Effective Prayer Life

Obviously, when the petty sins of my life were confessed and forgiven, I had a more effective prayer life. I sincerely believe that more of my prayers have been answered in the last four years than in any four-year period of my life. There has been no "second blessing" but a normal result following cleansing. Only a few times prior to the fasting experiences have I honestly, earnestly, sought to completely confess *all* the sins of my life. Fasting is not necessary to this kind of cleansing, but it is beneficial to me in these periods of waiting before the Lord.

During my first months of fasting and prayer God showed me the basic laws of ACTION, a Sunday School enrollment concept. These are stated in detail in *Where ACTION Is*[1] and *The ACTION Manual.*[2] Though these laws are elementary, they had been veiled from our view. I am confident that this information came to me in answer to prayer as I sought the keys that would unlock a growth era for my congregation.

As I examine my daily diary and reread the events that prompted the various fasts and the results of each, the experiences almost seem to be a series of miracles. One of these was a need for seven thousand dollars. The deadline was two weeks away. This payment kept hindering my ministry to others. I found myself spending considerable time thinking, planning, and worrying about how I would meet the obligation. My conscious burden for reaching the unreached was being overridden. This was not God's will. I fasted and prayed about the matter. The very hour I was led to cease my fast, I received a telephone call stating that the obligation had been satisfied. Instead of my having to make a payment, a payment would be made to me.

I Discovered a Previously Unknown Peace and Confidence

I am one of those fortunate persons who was born not too high strung or too low strung. I have ambition and drive, but not overly so. Therefore, though some things bother me, very few things have kept me awake at night or caused ulcers. However, once I came to the place in life where I was willing to turn everything over to the Lord, a new peace, unknown before, settled over my life. Things that once bothered me are no longer important. My goals and ambitions are higher now than ever before, but they are God-given rather than self-driven. He is responsible now and not me. I only make myself available for his use.

"In quietness and in confidence shall be your strength" (Isa. 30:15) is my philosophy. And why not? I believe that I am in the center of God's will and that his purpose is being worked out in the small details as well as the large ones. What a blessed place to be!

For over thirty years of marriage, my wife Eleanor and I have been separated only a few times. We need each other. Some marriage counselors would probably say we have an unhealthy marriage because where you see one of us, you see both. I rarely went out of town for a revival or Bible conference that Eleanor did not go with me. When the decision came for me to leave the pastorate and become the ACTION promotion specialist, and be away from home three-fourths of the year, we knew we needed the ministering hand of God on both of us. This could have been a crisis; instead, a "peace that passeth understanding" began to abide with us. Never a night passes that we do not talk with each other on the telephone. There our lives blend through the medium of electronics. How good God is; we might have lived in the day before the telephone.

I Have Found an Almost Unbelievable Strength To Overcome Temptations

"There hath no temptation taken you but such

as is common to man: but God is faithful, who
will not suffer you to be tempted above that ye
are able; but will, with the temptation also make
a way of escape" (1 Cor. 10:13). I illustrated this
marvelous truth earlier in the book. This is only
one of the many times I found additional strength.
Our strongest temptations are not necessarily in the
moral realm, but in the spiritual. If Satan can get
us to yield to the temptations to omit Bible reading,
practice short periods of prayer only, overlook devotional periods, and become so preoccupied we
have little or no time for others, he has destroyed
our vital witness.

The discipline and practice of fastings have in-
tensified these sacred times in my life. Some may
not need this discipline, but I do. For many years,
the first two hours of each day have been spent
with the Lord in a devotional study of his Word
and in prayer. These have been precious times. Of
course, there have been exceptions, as any pastor
knows.

One of my favorite Bible stories is found in
Judges 6—7. This is the story of Gideon. The dew
on Gideon's fleece was assurance of God's immediate presence. The dew sparkling on a man's life
is the credential of a person of God. Victory came
only after the dew-wetting. This was no ordinary,
commonplace experience but an extraordinary,
uncommon touch of God. The dew experience in
the garden only follows the blood experience. The
grace of salvation flows into the grace of manifestation. The dew experience expressed itself in the
conduct of Gideon's life. Many never enter into

the victor's circle because they never see the sparkle of the dew. It was at dewtime that Gideon found an unbelievable strength to overcome. This is my experience, too.

I Discover the Will of God More Easily

Upon seeing, for the first time, that the New Testament churches practiced fasting before and during the calling and ordaining of men (Acts 13:1-3; 14:23), I began to experiment with fasting in regard to discovering God's will for my life. On a number of occasions over the last few years, when the right decision was unclear, I discovered the answer following a fast. The fast has not been needed on every occasion, but I have not failed to make the right decision following a time of fasting.

Perhaps the greatest single decision in relation to my life's work came in the summer of 1975. I had served as a pastor for twenty-nine years.

As the information and excitement about ACTION began to spread throughout Florida (where I pastored), I worked out an agreement with Dr. Harold Bennett, executive secretary of the Florida Baptist Convention, and Dr. James Frost, Sunday School secretary of the Florida Baptist Convention, to interpret ACTION to all of the associations in the state.

About this time Dr. Frost shared the concept with the Sunday School leadership of the Southern Baptist Convention in Houston, Texas. A special committee from this group was formed to look into this new approach of enrolling people in Sunday

School. Dr. Frost, who had guided and encouraged me throughout the development of the plan, traveled with me to Nashville, where I met with this committee. Shortly after this Dr. Grady Cothen, president, and Dr. A. V. Washburn, Sunday School secretary, of the Baptist Sunday School Board, Nashville, Tennessee, invited me to become an employee of the Board to interpret ACTION nationwide. I did not know how I could do this, since my calling was to the pastorate. This was a momentous decision. I felt I was the pastor of the finest church in the world—a place I had served for nineteen years. Yet here was an opportunity to reach more people for Christ in one year than I could reach in a lifetime at Riverside. But I felt there was a deeper element in the decision: How could I, a pastor, change my life's work?

No matter how much I prayed and sought God's will during the following months, I could not discover God's will. I kept telling my wife, "Maybe later I will find it, but not now."

In the meantime, I was invited to present a testimony at Ridgecrest and Glorieta (denominational conference centers) where I spoke to over two thousand people each week for four weeks. ACTION exploded.

It seemed as though I had an invitation to every church in America. This added more pressure for a decision. My wife and I discussed the alternatives and prayed almost without ceasing, but no answer came. While I was at Glorieta the burden became almost unbearable. I began a fast while concentrating on the decision. About two days into the fast,

I took my Bible and strolled over to the prayer gardens. It was a quiet place in which one could almost hear the voice of God. After more than an hour of studying the Bible and praying, I came to a familiar passage in Exodus, chapters 3 and 4. Moses had spent forty years as a shepherd, but now God called him to a new field of service. I, too, had been a shepherd, a pastor, for almost thirty years. In these verses I saw God's will—he wanted me, like Moses, to go in a new direction. He promised to go with Moses to supply his every need, so he would go with me.

That evening I telephoned my wife. She was in Florida at our home, and I was in New Mexico. I opened my conversation with "Sweetheart, I have something to tell you. I've found God's will for us." She interrupted: "I know what you are about to tell me, for God gave me the answer today, also." Here we were, separated by thousands of miles; but God revealed his plan to both of us on the same day, about the same time of day. She then related how some circumstances at the church had been used to let her know what we needed to do. God moves in mysterious ways, but I'm convinced that it was only after I became desperate enough to seek God's face in a fast that he gave the answer.

8 A Few Cautions

I almost refused to write this book for fear that some would read it, be shallow in their understanding, and become unscripturally fanatical in their pursuit of a deeper life.

This chapter is to caution the reader to place fasting into a Spirit-led life. It is no less or no more important than almsgiving and prayer (Matt. 6:1-18).

Human nature is sinful and selfish. We have a tendency to lift up, talk about, and amplify the sensational, while minimizing the more important things of life.

Be Cautious with Your Health

I do not believe that fasting is for everyone. Christians with certain physical illnesses would aggravate these with extended fasts and therefore should seek medical advice before fasting. However, God instructed every Jew to fast one day a year on the Day of Atonement; so, obviously, this kind of fast should be all right for everyone in the twentieth century except the most critically ill.

Be Cautious with Your Attitude

Nothing is more obnoxious than someone who

talks about the same thing all the time—even if it is good.

I'm sure that health foods are good and should be considered, but most people involved with them will "drive you up the wall" talking about them.

This is true with some premillennialists. They seem to forget that there are dozens of other marvelous and helpful doctrines in God's Word. They make this doctrine a test of fellowship among the brethren. I am a premillennialist, but I can fellowship with, pray with, study with, work with, and go to heaven with those whose convictions differ from mine.

And then there are those who are hung up on certain religious words and sentences. These people slap you on the back and loudly exclaim, "Amen, brother, God bless you, my brother" or "Praise God, brother." If a child of God is impressed of the Holy Spirit to praise the Lord, he should do so. This is biblical. But repetitious words or sentences—even scriptural ones—will turn off those who need to be won.

My major concern in bringing up these illustrations is that God's people must be attractive and beautiful to the lost. Only after we get them to place their hands into ours can we place their hands in the nail-scarred hand of the Savior.

The person who fasts discovers an exhilarating experience and has the tendency to become a crusader for the cause. But we must remember the words of Jesus in Matthew 6, "Moreover when ye fast, be not, as the hypocrites, of a sad countenance: for they disfigure their faces, that they may appear unto men to fast. Verily I say unto you, They have their reward. But thou, when thou fastest, anoint thine head, and wash thy face; That thou appear not unto men to fast, but unto thy Father which is in secret: and thy Father, which seeth in secret, shall reward thee openly" (vv. 16-18). If this service becomes vocal, all heavenly reward is lost.

The holier-than-thou attitude is to be fought at all costs. The cause of Jesus Christ is injured by this attitude, for "there is none good but one" (Matt. 19:17).

Be honest in your fast; otherwise, a fast is a farce.

Be Cautious with Ritual

I grew up in a church where the Doxology was sung every Sunday. I have nothing against such a practice, except that soon it became a ritual and lost all of its meaning. Rituals do not have to lose their meaning, but they usually do.

Across the centuries several denominations have encouraged or required a partial or full-day fast one day each week. This has fallen into disrepute —it became a ritual. Ritual produces a shallowness, not earnestness.

My personal experience with fasting leads me away from a set time each week. Admittedly, the one-day-a-week fast has some merit and perhaps, to some, offsets the problems. But for me, I did not believe this was best.

The food shortage in the world has prompted many to omit a meal each week and donate the price of it to world food relief. This is noble but has nothing to do with the subject of the spiritual fast except as it applies to Isaiah 58:6.

Be Cautious of a Substitute

Since the New Testament days there has been a contrast between salvation by grace alone and salvation by works. This word of caution is expressed to remind the reader that salvation cannot be achieved, even by fasting. It is achieved only through a personal faith in Jesus Christ.

People who fast for great lengths of time begin to hallucinate, to see visions of grandeur. Several false religions have been started under such spells. For instance, the Koran was written during a fast. The experience of Jesus in Matthew 4 warns us of this possibility. After Jesus had fasted forty days and forty nights, Satan came to tempt him. Not only did he deal with Jesus in a physical temptation: "Command that these stones be made bread" (v. 3) but also in an emotional or psychological temptation: "Cast thyself down . . . He shall give His angels charge concerning thee: and in their hands they shall bear thee up, lest at any time thou dash thy foot against a stone" (v.6). Also, and this is very important, in a religious temptation, Satan said, "All these things will I give thee" (v. 9). We discover in these verses that during a fast we may be tempted physically, emotionally, psychologically, or religiously. This is why Jesus resisted the tempter with quotations from the Bible—"It is written . . ." (v. 10). The fast-er should spend much time studying the Bible during a fast.

Be Cautious of Self-deception

Fasting is a time of utmost honesty. Its purpose is to dig out the sins that have been hidden—to sincerely evaluate one's standing with God.

But since fasting is done in secret, it is fraught with the problems of self-deceit. Since no other human being is available to observe the motives, it is easy to disguise them. Though it seems unthinkable that a person would deceive himself during such a time, do not forget Satan's presence. He is the great deceiver.

Notes

Introduction

1. Andrew Murray, *With Christ in the School of Prayer* (Old Tappan, New Jersey: Fleming Revell Co., 1975).
2. Andrew Murray, *Full and Joyous Surrender* (Westchester, Illinois: Good New Publishers, 1959).
3. R. A. Torrey, *How to Pray* (Chicago, Illinois: Moody Press).
4. *Ibid.*
5. *Ibid.*
6. John Wesley, *The Journal of John Wesley* (Chicago, Illinois: Moody Press).
7. O. Hallesby, *Prayer* (Minneapolis, Minnesota: Augsburg Publishing House, 1931, Revised 1959).
8. Basil Miller, *Charles G. Finney* (Grand Rapids, Michigan: Zondervan Publishing House, 1941).
9. Roland Bainton, *Here I Stand* (New York: Abingdon Press).
10. Henry Martyn.
11. E. M. Bounds, *Power Through Prayer* (Chicago, Illinois: Moody Press).

Chapter 2

1. Allan Cott, M.D., *Fasting; the Ultimate Diet* (New York: Bantam Books, Inc., 1975).
2. Otto H. F. Buchinger, M.D., *Everything You Want to Know About Fasting* (New York: Pyramid Books, 1972).

Suggested Reading

Bailey, Faith Coxe, *Adoniram Judson*. Chicago: Moody Press.

Bainton, Roland H. *Here I Stand*. New York and Nashville: Abingdon Press.

Beall, James Lee, *The Adventure of Fasting*. Old Tappan, N.J.: Fleming H. Revell.

Blessitt, Arthur, *Forty Days at the Cross*. Nashville: Broadman Press.

Bounds, E. M. *Power Through Prayer*. Chicago: Moody Press.

Bragg, Paul C. *The Miracle of Fasting*. Santa Ana, California: Health Science.

Buckinger, Otto H. F. *Everything You Want to Know About Fasting*. New York: Pyramid Books.

Carter, Charles W., Ed. *Wesleyan Bible Commentary*, Grand Rapids, Michigan: William B. Eerdman's, Vol. I.

Cott, Allan. *Fasting: The Ultimate Diet*. New York: Bantam Books.

Dunn, James M., Loring, Ben E., Jr., and Strickland, Phil D. *Endangered Species*. Nashville: Broadman Press.

Hallesby, O. *Prayer*. Minneapolis, Minnesota: Augsburg Publishing House.

Kirban, Salem. *How to Keep Healthy and Happy*

by Fasting. Huntingdon Road, Pennsylvania: Salem Kirban.

Lloyd-Jones, D. Martyn. *Studies in the Sermon on the Mount.* Old Tappan, N.J.: Fleming H. Revell.

Miller, Basil. *Charles G. Finney.* Grand Rapids, Michigan: Zondervan Publishing House.

Murray, Andrew. *With Christ in the School of Prayer.* Old Tappan, N.J.: Fleming H. Revell.

————. *Absolute Surrender.* Chicago: Moody Press.

Prince, Derek. *Shaping History Through Prayer and Fasting.* Tappan, N.J.: Fleming H. Revell.

Shelton, Herbert M. *Fasting Can Save Your Life.* Chicago: Natural Hygiene Press.

Simon, Arthur. *Bread for the World.* New York: Paulist Press and William B. Eerdman's.

Torrey, R. A. *How to Pray.* Old Tappan: Fleming H. Revell.

Wallis, Arthur. *God's Chosen Fast.* Fort Washington, Pennsylvania: Christian Literature Crusade.

Wesley, John. *The Journal of John Wesley.* Chicago: Moody Press.